SISTER AND LOVERS

DRAMA SERIES 21

Canadä

Guernica Editions Inc. acknowledges the financial support of the
Government of Canada through the Book Publishing Industry Development
Program (BPIDP).

MARIO FRATTI

SISTER AND LOVERS

TWO PLAYS

GUERNICA
TORONTO·BUFFALO·LANCASTER (U.K.)
2001

Mario Fratti is represented by Samuel French, Inc. 45 West 25th Street,
New York, N.Y. 10010 U.S.A.

Antonio D'Alfonso, editor
Guernica Editions Inc.
P.O. Box 117, Station P, Toronto (ON), Canada M5S 2S6
2250 Military Road, Tonawanda, N.Y. 14150-6000 U.S.A.
Gazelle, Falcon House, Queen Square, Lancaster LA1 1RN U.K.

Typeset by Selina.
Printed in Canada.
First edition.

Legal Deposit – Fourth Quarter
National Library of Canada
Library of Congress Catalog Card Number: 2001095238
National Library of Canada Cataloguin in Publication Data
Fratti, Mario
Sister ; and, Lovers
(Drama series ; 21)
Two plays.
ISBN 1-55071-150-4
I. Title. II. Title: Lovers. III. Series.
PR9120.9.F7S5 2001 852'.914 C2001-902459-2

CONTENTS

TWO PLAYS BY MARIO FRATTI

The structure of Mario Fratti's plays is spare, cut to the bone, omitting internal exposition, secondary plots and nearly all stage directions that are used to cue both readers and spectators to a playwright's intentions. To the contrary, Fratti's plays typically resemble brief working scripts. One need only compare the printed version of a play written at the turn of the century by, say, George Bernard Shaw to see Fratti's pared down mode. He long ago abandoned the conventions of a well-made play to concentrate on dramatizing an event with a strict economy of means. The curtain goes up on an action already begun and falls before the audience has quite caught its breath – Fratti's trademark is the final knockout punch. Its after-shock lingers until after the spectator has left the theater, just as meanings often resonate after a reader has laid aside a text. Nothing has been explained, yet expectations have been reversed, those of the protagonist and of the audience as well.

The method suits Fratti's sense of mission to communicate with an audience directly, not only without rhetoric, but through simple situations. Indeed, Fratti sees drama not as an artifice or a literary construct so much as an opportunity to teach his audience how to think twice about social dilemmas – especially those arising out of the complexities of gender, the dynamics of family, the changing mood on the sexual battlefield. He turns a cold eye on small actions that come to seem symptomatic of contemporary manners and mores: characters who appear to be candid reveal their motivation by hidden agendas; intimate relationships fall apart as the principals jockey for advantage; language operates as a smoke screen and a tool for a clever manipulator. As may be inferred, then, the two works in this volume are problem plays in the tradition of satirizing human folly in order to awaken a dormant consciousness.

Fratti shares with other Italian American writers a concern with preserving family. In *Sister,* a young man afflicted with a sexual double standard condemns his sister for promiscuity while exonerating himself for similar behavior. Responding self-righteously to his mother's queries about his relations with women, he clings to his mask of machismo which equates love with sex. Eventually, a shocking discovery about his parentage causes a change of heart and he shows himself capable of accepting human frailties, his own and those of others. Arrogance gives way to something like humility and delusion to enlightenment.

Differently, today's appetite for exposés about sexual behavior provides a backdrop for *Lovers,* an ironic title for a thriller plot about loveless coupling. A timid wife in her first lesbian affair finds herself in a hellish web of jealousies instead of the benign sisterhood she imagined. Her confused yet obliging husband offers the lovers security in a *ménage à trois,* but to the wife's horror, her lover finds a way to kill him. Complications, false leads, a double cross, and a culminating recital of twisted motives follow as the killer's former lesbian lover, a detective, appears with professional advice about how to cover up the crime. At the least, the unworldly young wife and the audience both learn that violence obeys no gender boundaries.

Mario Fratti has written more than seventy plays in Italian and English. These have been translated and produced around the globe, and have won countless drama prizes and a following among popular audiences as well. His prolific output shows no sign of diminishing as he also continues to lecture worldwide, write reviews, sponsor budding playwrights, produce a theater series, and serve as a generous guide to the professional theater community.

Nina daVinci Nichols
Rutgers University

SISTER

Characters

Mother (Margherita): a beautiful woman, fifty-nine.
Daughter (Rosanna): a beautiful woman, thirty-nine.
Son (Carlo): a handsome young man, twenty.

The Place: Today in New York.

ACT ONE

A living room. The mother is embroidering. She observes the daughter who is admiring herself and her attire in the mirror; she strokes her eyebrows, fixes her lipstick; she wants to be beautiful and elegant because she is getting ready for a date.

MOTHER *(after observing her for a long time)*: What time are you coming back?

DAUGHTER: Tomorrow. Noonish. Maybe . . . *(A silence.)*

MOTHER: Who is it this time?

DAUGHTER: You don't know him.

MOTHER: Is he married?

DAUGHTER: I don't know.

MOTHER *(after a silence)*: How long have you known him?

DAUGHTER: Just a few days.

MOTHER: You didn't have a chance to ask him?

DAUGHTER: You don't ask on your first date.

MOTHER: When do you ask? On the third date? On the fifth? When?

DAUGHTER *(while she's adding the last touches to her face)*: He lives alone.

MOTHER: Does it look like a bachelor's apartment?

DAUGHTER: What does a bachelor's apartment look like?

MOTHER (timidly): It's easy to understand if a man . . .

DAUGHTER *(interrupting her)*: He's not married, if that's what makes you happy.

MOTHER: Do you cook for him?

DAUGHTER: No. He likes to eat out. We always have breakfast and lunch out.

MOTHER: Is there any hope with this one?

DAUGHTER: No. It is what it is. Now.

MOTHER: They say that at your age . . .

DAUGHTER (*bored, interrupting again*): I know, I know.

MOTHER (*continuing*): . . . It's very difficult to find a husband.

DAUGHTER: I'm not looking for a husband.

MOTHER: What are you looking for? What do you want?

DAUGHTER: Nothing. To live day by day. After eight hours in the office, I need . . . (*A vague gesture.*)

MOTHER: You need what?

DAUGHTER: Distraction. Fun. I have a right to relax, to forget.

MOTHER: What do you want to forget?

DAUGHTER (*looking at her ironically*): You're asking me?

MOTHER: We all have some disappointments. One, two . . .

DAUGHTER: One hundred.

MOTHER: It doesn't matter. Every disappointment makes you stronger. One learns.

DAUGHTER (*ironically, fixing her lipstick*): You learn what? To hate them?

MOTHER: Why do you speak like that? Why are you always so bitter?

DAUGHTER: Because my life is no fun. I'm almost forty and I have come back here in this same old house to live with you. (*Ironic.*) With my sweet Mommy.

MOTHER: Look on the positive side of things. You live here with us, in the heart of the city.

DAUGHTER *(ironic)*: Ha!

MOTHER: You can't deny that it's very convenient for you. A stone's throw from your office.

DAUGHTER *(ironic)*: I don't deny that.

MOTHER: You're not paying rent.

DAUGHTER *(aggressive)*: I was waiting for that! How much do you want a month? A week? Or let's say, every fifteen days, that's better. They pay me every two weeks, you know! You always check my mail. Sometimes you even open my letters . . . *(with heavy irony)* . . . "by mistake!"

MOTHER *(ignoring this accusation)*: Believe me, I mention the rent only because . . .

DAUGHTER *(cutting)*: You mentioned it because it's on your mind. How much do you want?

MOTHER: Nothing, absolutely nothing! I only want you to be happy.

DAUGHTER: It's too late, according to that newspaper. I read it too. *(Slightly ironic.)* I've only two chances out of one hundred to find a husband. And where do you find the jerk who marries you after . . .

MOTHER: After what?

DAUGHTER: One thousand encounters with the bastards who live in this city.

MOTHER: Shh . . . Don't talk like that! *(Looking at the door from which her son might enter.)* You confuse him, you irritate him, you wound him.

DAUGHTER: It's none of his business!

MOTHER: He's jealous.

DAUGHTER: What right has he got to be jealous?

MOTHER: You know.

DAUGHTER: No, I don't know. He should look for a better paying job.

MOTHER: He's confused, upset. And your behavior does not help.

DAUGHTER: What behavior?

MOTHER: What you do. Your life.

DAUGHTER: It is my life!

MOTHER: But it is tied to his life, to ours.

DAUGHTER: We are three islands. You, him, me. And everybody should mind his own business!

MOTHER: We are not three islands. We are a family.

DAUGHTER (*ironically*): Very nice family!

MOTHER: We sit at the same table.

DAUGHTER: Once a year!

MOTHER: On Sundays, on holidays.

DAUGHTER: What holidays! We have nothing to celebrate!

MOTHER: Religious holidays. You are the one who is trying to avoid them. Pretending to be very busy.

DAUGHTER (*surprised*): Pretending?

MOTHER: Yes. You are always in a rush, and you tell us you're always very busy.

DAUGHTER: I am, I am!

MOTHER: What I mean is, you're always running somewhere.

DAUGHTER: I'm running, yes. Running away from your questions, from his questions.

MOTHER: He has not been asking any lately.

DAUGHTER: I wish that were true!

MOTHER: It is true. In the past, he wanted to know everything. Now . . .

DAUGHTER: Now?

MOTHER: Maybe he has given up.

DAUGHTER: It's high time.

MOTHER: Maybe he understood.

DAUGHTER: Understands what?

MOTHER: That . . . *(the daughter is waiting for an explanation)* . . . That it is futile with you.

DAUGHTER: Futile? What's futile about me?

MOTHER: That you are a rebel and we can do nothing to change you.

DAUGHTER: To change me? At my age?

MOTHER: It's impossible to stop you, to try . . .

DAUGHTER: To stop me? To prevent me from living? Like you? You stopped living, when father left you! Not me! I want to live my life now! You're both crazy to think I'll change.

(We hear steps. The son enters.)

SON *(to the two women)*: Hi!

MOTHER: Hello.

(The daughter ignores him. He approaches her and observes her with curiosity. A silence.)

SON: Are you going out again?

(The daughter looks at the mother ironically, as if she wanted to say: "Do you see? He has not changed!")

DAUGHTER *(looking at him defiantly)*: Yes. I'm going out again.

SON: Where are you going?

DAUGHTER: You too? I told Mother I'm going to Anita's.

SON: What time are you coming back?

DAUGHTER: Mind your own business.

SON *(insisting)*: What time?

DAUGHTER: Maybe at midnight, maybe tomorrow. We're going dancing.

SON: Hunting.

DAUGHTER *(insisting)*: Dancing. You are the one who goes hunting. Not me.

SON *(to the mother)*: Who is Anita?

MOTHER: A co-worker.

DAUGHTER *(ready to leave)*: Good-bye!

MOTHER: Come home soon. Take a taxi. It's dangerous at night.

DAUGHTER *(exiting)*: I know, I know.

(She exits. A silence. The son begins whistling, without being aware of it. The mother continues embroidering. The son is very nervous and takes a magazine; throws it on the table; takes a book, leafs through it; slaps it on the table; he is irritable.)

SON: Where is she going?

MOTHER: *(defending her)*: She works all day long, a difficult boring job.

SON: Who is she going with?

MOTHER: She told you. A friend of hers. They're entitled to . . . *(a vague gesture)* . . .

SON: To what?

MOTHER: Some relaxation, dinner, dancing . . .

SON: You know perfectly well where she's going.

MOTHER *(pretending to be surprised)*: Where? What do you know about it?

SON: I know everything.

MOTHER *(with curiosity)*: Everything . . . What do you mean?

SON: You're my mother. I can't give you such details. You know too.

MOTHER: She's thirty-nine. She has been unlucky.

SON: The usual story.

MOTHER: A great love when she was sixteen. A nice man who adored her . . .

SON (*skeptical*): Adored her? If he adored her, why did he disappear? Why?

MOTHER: He was very young. Younger than you. He was afraid of a great love, a commitment. A tie for life. You'd have done the same thing.

SON: When? In what situation?

(*The mother studies him.*)

MOTHER: You've already had girlfriends. Why did you leave them?

SON (*after a brief pause*): I was disappointed.

MOTHER: What do you mean? What does "disappointed" mean?

SON: They were superficial.

MOTHER: In what sense?

SON: Mother! Why are you so curious?

MOTHER: I just want to understand. What does "disappointing" mean?

SON: It's obvious. You like some people, you don't like others.

MOTHER: Tell me about it. If you like initially . . .

SON: Then they reveal themselves.

MOTHER: What do they reveal?

SON (*impatient and reluctant*): You know, Mother. Some are ambitious. Others are rather stupid.

MOTHER: Tell me about your lovers.

SON: "Lovers?" What a big word for a saintly woman like you!

MOTHER: Why did you leave them? The first, the second . . .

SON (*hesitating*): Anna was pedantic.

MOTHER: Was she too cultured for you?

SON (*ignoring*): Mary was unnerving.

MOTHER: You're intolerant.

SON (*continuing*): Nancy was difficult.

MOTHER: Harsh words. Pedantic, unnerving, difficult. So you just dismissed them. You are cruel.

SON: How can I make myself clearer? If one is difficult . . . you know what it means.

MOTHER: No. I belong to another generation. What does "difficult" mean today?

SON: It means what it meant yesterday. If you go with a woman, you want to be happy, serene. No problems.

MOTHER: She must therefore . . .

SON: Behave herself.

MOTHER: What do you mean "behave herself?" Behavior changes constantly. A woman sees, feels, reacts to your behavior. How do you behave? What do you want from her?

SON (*trying to avoid the subject*): Mother . . .

MOTHER: I want to know. What do you want from a woman?

SON: I'm really not comfortable talking to you about this . . .

MOTHER: I've also been a wife.

SON (*evasive*): I'm sure you were an angel with Dad, but you also . . .

MOTHER (*with some sadness*): I was sixteen, it's true, I was an angel. Full of trust, gentle, loving, obedient. Is that what you want?

SON: Not precisely. Everything was simpler then. It was easy for you to be the way you are.

MOTHER (*ironic*): It wasn't so easy. To be "obedient?"

SON: That's an interesting admission. You pretended

to be an angel. *(Indicating the door from which the daughter exited.)* Same blood. Like mother like daughter.

MOTHER *(ignoring the allusion to her daughter)*: I was controlling myself.

SON: Were you lying?

MOTHER: At times . . . if it was necessary.

SON: "Necessary?" In what situation, for instance?

MOTHER: To calm him, to placate him.

SON: You see? You knew how to behave. And Dad was happy. I remember that. He was happy with you, with Rosanna, with me. You didn't give him any problems.

MOTHER *(with curiosity)*: What problems do you have with your lovers . . . *(correcting herself)* . . . your girlfriends?

SON: How come you are so interested?

MOTHER: We never speak about this. We should. I want to understand.

SON: Understand what?

MOTHER: As you were saying before. With a couple of words you dismiss a human being: "pedantic, unnerving, difficult." And you close the chapter.

SON: If it's true, it's true.

MOTHER: Quick and cruel judgments. Why don't you give your women time to grow with you, to understand you better? Why do you abandon them, ignore them?

SON *(surprised by this unusual passion)*: You are in a strange mood today. How come?

MOTHER: Maybe I'm tired of controlling myself. I want to know.

SON: To know what?

MOTHER: Hundreds of things. What do you want from a woman? What did you want from Anna? from Mary? from Nancy?

SON: Okay. Let's proceed with some order. Anna . . . beautiful hands . . . beautiful face . . . a warm smile. I fell in love right away. We had the same tastes, more or less . . . ballet, opera, theatre . . . but she was incredibly pedantic. It was a pain to go out with her . . . she knew everything. Bios of the dancers, history of the operas, lists of the plays written by Tom, Dick and Harry, comparisons, parallels, critical comments. I felt like vomiting. And she was always implying a reproach. "How come you don't know this? Don't you ever read? Aren't you interested in politics? Who is the president of Senegal or of Zimbabwe?" Who gives a damn? What's the difference if an opera was written in 1890 or in 1927? Who cares if the librettist and the composer were quarreling all the time? Relax, enjoy your life! Stop tormenting your neighbor! I go to see an opera to amuse myself, not to suffer at the thought of my ignorance! I don't want to be constantly reminded that we ignore 99% of human knowledge.

MOTHER (*almost to herself*): Maybe it would have been better if she hadn't read so many books and learned so much. (*She stares at him.*)

SON: And besides, she was always around, she always needed something from me!

MOTHER: Weren't you moved by that need, by her love?

SON: No. It would have been better if she had "controlled" herself, as you did. A man can't live with a woman who obsesses him with an avalanche of information, facts, dates, ideas. One goes to school if he wants to memorize and suffer. In life, one wants to have fun, joy, to relax! Life should be a constant holiday.

MOTHER: It is not a holiday.

SON: A relationship should be a constant joy. Couples should be at ease with each other. One doesn't choose an enemy, in life; one chooses a companion. *Cum pane* one who shares bread with you. One who thinks like you!

MOTHER *(ironically)*: A soulmate!

SON: If possible, why not? I'm looking for that!

MOTHER: Mary. Why did you leave her?

SON *(with a gesture of annoyance)*: That one . . .

MOTHER: "Unnerving," you said.

SON: She was meticulous. *(Imitating her.)* You should see how she ate. In a very affected manner! "Fix your necktie," "buy a new shirt," "you need a dinner jacket," "those nails . . . ," "those shoes . . ." She was looking for perfection. She needed me to be impeccable, perfect in any circumstance. I hate those with obsessive needs. What did she want from me? To be my mother? My teacher? No, thank you! I don't want another mother who is trying to correct me, to change me!

MOTHER: Me? Have I ever tried to change you?

SON *(ignoring)*: I am what I am! I hate neckties, shiny shoes, hypocrisy! She was a hypocrite! That's why I dumped her!

MOTHER: "Dumped," as if she were a thing, a rag.

SON: I'm not the one who invented that expression!

MOTHER: You left her. Alone and weeping.

SON: Weeping? that one? She is probably obsessing some other poor devil.

MOTHER: You said that Nancy was difficult. What do you mean by difficult?

SON: Complicated. This is good, that is no good. Proteins, calories, doctors, weight, fears. Avoid meat, avoid ice-creams, no cakes, no coffee. And then, all her doubts . . . She always needed me, to help her decide. Should I buy this? Today or tomorrow? Maybe tomorrow. A procrastinator. The champion of all procrastinators.

MOTHER: What did she pro- . . . ? What did she postpone?

SON: Everything.

MOTHER (*cautiously, after a pause*): Should a woman . . . always be "ready" to . . . ?

SON (*surprised by such a question*): To do what?

MOTHER: You know. You were angry because she was difficult, always undecided, the person who says "maybe, later, tomorrow, the day after tomorrow," all because she didn't . . . ? You men, do you prefer a woman to be always ready to . . . ? (*She does not finish the sentence.*)

SON: No, I was not talking about "that."

MOTHER: Don't change the subject. We are talking about "that." I'm trying to understand you men.

SON (*smiling*): At your age, mother?

MOTHER: Better late than never. Do you want your woman to be always at your disposal? When you want it?

SON: Mother, you should not be talking about these things.

MOTHER: Why not?

SON (*smiling, with a sense of humor*): Mothers are "sacred." They know nothing about . . . they don't do those things.

MOTHER: Oh no? It's time we talk about it. Finally!

SON: Watch TV if you want sex-education! Don't ask your son for God's sake!

MOTHER: I want to know from you. Tell me. What do men want? Should a woman be hard to get?

SON (*vague*): Not really . . .

MOTHER (*insisting*): Should she be . . . (*cannot find the right word*) . . . open? (*She corrects herself.*) I mean . . . ready for that?

SON: That theory is false.

MOTHER (*surprised*): False?

SON: If you really want to know, the contrary is true.

MOTHER (*with curiosity*): The contrary?

SON: Men prefer a woman who is not interested only in that, always in "that." If she is too aggressive, she makes her man uneasy.

MOTHER (*reflecting*): Interesting. (*Repeating it to herself.*) It's better if she is not always ready. It's better if she's not aggressive. When you said "difficult," you meant sexually.

SON: No, I told you, when I said that Nancy was difficult, I meant . . . (*looking for the words*) meticulous, fussy, complicated.

MOTHER (*reflecting; speaking almost to herself*): The idea would be then to be simple, passive, accepting, a martyr.

SON: Not precisely. Let's be open about this. Put yourself into the shoes of a man who traveled two hours from home to his office and vice versa. The perennial commuter! You've been arguing for eight or nine hours with your boss and colleagues who ask for the impossible. You come back home, you want peace. You need tranquillity. A silent comfortable home. Complete absence of new obsessive problems.

MOTHER: A mute wife.

SON: For an hour, at least. Until I catch my breath.

MOTHER (*ironically*): And when you break your silence, then she's allowed to talk.

SON: Exactly. She must be intelligent, understanding, tolerant.

MOTHER: "Tolerant." She must "tolerate" your shortcomings.

SON: They're not really shortcomings. They are needs. She must understand my needs: silence, peace, happiness.

MOTHER (*still vaguely ironic*): While the poor girl . . .

SON: The poor girl what?

MOTHER: What about her shortcomings, her needs?

SON: She can talk about them, of course. At the opportune moment. Didn't you talk to Dad?

MOTHER: Now and then, when he was in a good mood.

SON: You see? You understood when it was the right time to talk, when it was opportune to be silent.

MOTHER: Are men different from women?

SON: Of course we are.

MOTHER: Do they have different needs?

SON: In a sense.

MOTHER: A need for peace, tranquillity, serenity?

SON: Those are the same.

MOTHER: A need to talk, to communicate?

SON: Sure.

MOTHER: What are the fundamental differences?

SON: We are not speaking about the physical ones of course. A man has a cross to bear. He must provide for his family. The life of a woman is much easier.

MOTHER *(ironically)*: Easier?

SON *(continuing)*: To take care of the house . . .

MOTHER *(intervening, with irony)*: To obey her husband.

SON: It's not a question of obeying, it's a question of "understanding him." It's a jungle out there: the home must be an oasis of peace and joy.

MOTHER: Women heard the news. More than 70% are out there, in that jungle. They work.

SON: Those are different cases. If they work, they are equal to me, to men.

MOTHER: Same rights and needs?

SON: The same.

MOTHER: She comes home very tired.

SON *(completing the sentence)*: She's entitled to at least one hour of silence. The same hour I demand. Absolute parity. An oasis of happiness.

MOTHER: Who's taking care of the "oasis?" Who cooks?

SON: Two salaries. Then there's money for help. A maid.

MOTHER *(correcting him)*: Domestic collaboration.

SON: Call it whatever you want.

MOTHER: And this "collaborator" will take care of the children, the kitchen, the cleaning of the house . . .

SON: An ideal situation!

MOTHER: And when this help is not there? You can't

pay her twenty-four hours a day. Who's taking care of the house?

SON: Husband and wife can take turns. They can discuss all the details. A loving collaboration.

MOTHER: Then you believe in discussion?

SON: Of course. Did you doubt that?

MOTHER: With your three girlfriends, did you ever discuss future?

SON: No.

MOTHER: Why not?

SON: I never contemplated a future with them. *(A silence. The mother studies him.)*

MOTHER: Why did you court them?

SON: Because it's natural to experiment. To enjoy each other.

MOTHER: At their expense?

SON: What do you mean? Pleasure for me means pleasure for them too.

MOTHER: And after you have . . . *(looks for the right word)* . . . conquered them, you say good-bye!

SON: Why not? If they're not on your level.

MOTHER: What do you mean by level?

SON: If they don't fulfill my dreams.

MOTHER: What about their dreams?

SON: You should know that very often it's the woman who leaves the man – who dumps him – because she feels they're not compatible. They all want a prince charming.

(Telephone rings. The mother lifts the receiver, listens.)

MOTHER: No, no one with that name lives here. Wrong number. *(Hangs the receiver up.)*

MOTHER *(with sadness)*: Why are men deceitful?

SON: Who says they are deceitful?

MOTHER: I read it in a magazine. "Men lie, pretend to love, to have what you call 'pleasure.' Women give their bodies in the hope of being loved." They only want love.

SON (*ironically*): "Those poor women!" I don't lie. I always speak clearly. I put all my cards on the table. I'm not interested in marriage. They know it.

MOTHER: Why do you flatter them? Why do you give them hopes, cruelly, and then . . . ?

SON: What hopes? I don't delude anyone. Never!

MOTHER (*insisting*): Why do you lie? they won't stay with you if they don't feel loved, desired.

SON: When it's over, it's over. We cannot love them all.

MOTHER: But you can desire them.

SON: It's a biological law. It doesn't depend on us, in a sense, our brains, our reason. It's an uncontrollable instinct. Chemistry, desire.
(Telephone rings again. The mother hurries to pick up the receiver.)

MOTHER: No, wrong number. (*Hangs up the receiver.*)

SON (*after a silence full of suspicion and curiosity*): Who was it?

MOTHER: Wrong number.

SON: Who did he want?

MOTHER (*vague, lying*): A certain . . . Violet.
(The son gets up and places himself near the telephone. He is suspicious and he is ready to answer if it rings again.)

MOTHER (*surprising him*): Why are you afraid of women?

SON (*surprised*): Afraid? Not me!

MOTHER: Are you afraid you can't satisfy them?

SON (*in a tone of reproach*): Mother, where are you getting these ideas? What kind of talk is this?

MOTHER: Answer. Why do you have that fear? We are not interested in what you think. Tenderness can make us just as happy.

SON (*moved, surprised, cautious*): Years ago . . . you didn't know much, you didn't want much.

MOTHER: And now? What do we know now?

SON: Not you . . . (*He is ill at ease; he doesn't like the subject.*) Women . . . other women . . . the young ones . . . (*He hesitates.*)

MOTHER: The young ones keep talking.

SON: Those of my generation, they know everything. They want everything.

MOTHER: Tell me.

SON: Mother, there are some new words that you've never heard . . .

MOTHER: I know them all now. What are you afraid of? Why did you leave your first woman? The second? The third? Because they wanted too much?

SON (*uneasy*): Mother . . .

MOTHER: I am a woman. Same blood. Family. Speak to me. Talk.

SON: It's not so easy. In my case, I got bored with them. Something was missing.

MOTHER: What was missing?

SON: That spark that there was at the beginning between you and Dad. (*He stares at her. He would like a confirmation.*) Only at the beginning . . . for a few years . . . then . . .

MOTHER: Then?

SON: I don't know. You know what happened . . . What happened?

MOTHER: He didn't come back home. He disappeared. That's all.

SON *(cautiously)*: Why? Maybe . . .

MOTHER: Was it my fault? *(She reflects for a moment, uncertain.)* Maybe. I was too much in love. But let's go back to your women. The young ones, your generation. Do they want too much?

SON *(uncertain, admitting)*: I speak to my friends. We confide. Yes, there are women who know too much, who want too much.

MOTHER: Isn't that better if they "know?"

SON: No. The less she knows the better it is.

MOTHER *(surprised and fascinated by this thesis)*: That's a fascinating confession. "The less she knows the better it is." Why?

SON *(uncertain)*: It means that she didn't have too many experiences.

MOTHER: And you prefer that?

SON: In a sense.

MOTHER: Do you prefer it or not?

SON: I prefer it.

MOTHER *(ironically)*: It's obvious, isn't it? The less she knows the more you can teach her. The way you want her to be. Lover and teacher. It's a dream many people have. All men, maybe.

(The telephone rings again. The son is very quick this time, he picks up the receiver and listens. Mother is tense and nervous.)

SON *(on the phone after listening)*: No. She's not here . . . she went out . . . I don't know . . . Who am I? Why do you want to know? . . . Yes, yes, I'm her little brother. But you, how do you know? Did we ever meet? . . . Where? . . . How? . . . Who are you? . . . Did you call before? . . . Oh yes! Leave her alone! (*Slams the receiver down; stares at the Mother; a silence.*)

SON (*to Mother*): He called before. Why did you lie?

MOTHER: You're always so jealous.

SON: One of her lovers?

MOTHER: Why are you so jealous?

SON: Who is that clown?

MOTHER: Why do you call him a clown?

SON: He was uncertain and creepy. Icky. Who is he?

MOTHER: An old friend. She doesn't want to see him any longer. That's why I said: "Wrong number." I hoped he would understand.

SON: Since when has he been calling?

MOTHER: Years.

SON: Why doesn't she want to see him?

MOTHER: As you said before "Love passes." She's probably tired of him. She finds him . . . boring.

SON: Who's she seeing now?

MOTHER: I don't know. (*A silence. She looks at Son; she studies him.*) Why are you so jealous?

SON: I don't know.

MOTHER: Why don't you learn to accept?

SON: To accept what?

MOTHER: That she's free, like you. It's her life. Shouldn't we care about her?

SON: She's your daughter, she's my sister.

MOTHER: It's not easy for a lonely woman . . . You described your philosophy before. You stated that men are fickle. Today it's yes, tomorrow it's no.

SON: She should know that too. She should have learned that by now.

MOTHER: She knows. What bothers her is your jealousy. She always asks me why "Why is he so jealous?"

SON: Instinct. It's our house, it's our blood. Our family. I want to protect her.

MOTHER: She also has a right to live.

SON: Do you call that a life?

MOTHER: Men don't speak clearly, they don't say that they only want, they are not honest.

SON: At her age, she should know this.

MOTHER: A woman is always hoping for some tenderness. She hopes. She trusts. She's confused. I am confused too. If Rosanna knew, for instance, that you men prefer "to teach," she would pretend she's innocent.

SON (*vaguely ironically*): "She would pretend?"

MOTHER: This is what you want, isn't it?

SON: She wouldn't know how, she couldn't. She's a rebel. I saw how she treats people. She is impatient, intolerant, aggressive.

MOTHER: Independent. Men should respect and admire an independent woman, someone who is self-sufficient.

SON: Independent up to a point. She gives orders. To me too.

MOTHER: It's her character.

SON: A man cannot accept a woman with that kind of character. She screams, she shouts, she threatens. She tries to intimidate me "giving me orders."

MOTHER: She's almost twenty years older than you.

SON: So what? I am the man of the house. It's up to me to give orders.

MOTHER (*with some sadness*): That's what he used to say.

SON: Dad. Tell me. Why did he leave us?

MOTHER (*after a silence, hesitating*): I don't know, I haven't understood why . . .

SON (*after a short pause, studying her*): What kind of mistakes did you make?

MOTHER: You see? Your first reaction is that it had to be the woman who made mistakes.

SON: Both of you maybe . . .

MOTHER: "Maybe."

SON (*correcting himself*): Indeed. There's always blame on both sides. Even I am to blame.

MOTHER (*reflecting with sadness*): Yes. Maybe I made some mistakes . . . He had some shortcomings.

SON: Tell me about his shortcomings. Maybe I inherited some of them.

MOTHER: He was always suspicious. He used to say: "When the husband is not around, the woman deceives and lies. What did you do today?"

SON: He was obviously joking. He had a sense of humor.

MOTHER: Another one of his "jokes." "When you come home, beat your wife; you don't know what she did. She does."

SON: Those are just old proverbs handed down from father to son.

MOTHER: Do you believe in those proverbs?

SON: No. Did he ever strike you? (*A silence.*)

MOTHER: Seldom.

SON: That is?

MOTHER (*reluctant*): Once a month, maybe . . . (*A silence.*)

SON: And you accepted that? Without reacting?

MOTHER: I loved him. He was very jealous. But I

understood. I was moved by that . . . (*trying to justify herself*) . . . I was proud too . . . I was his "property." He often used that word. For him, marriage was a contract.

SON (*ironically*): Nice word!

MOTHER: A purchase contract. And if I tried to tell him that a contract has two signatures, two commitments, he used to whistle.

SON (*surprised, becoming aware that he has that habit too*): Why did he whistle?

MOTHER: He always whistled when he was angry. It was his way to warn me that he was about to explode.

SON: Was he often angry?

MOTHER: Often.

SON: With you?

MOTHER: With the world. He felt exploited, used, betrayed. And he wanted revenge.

SON: On whom? On what?

MOTHER: Society. Those who underpaid him and deprived him of his dreams.

SON: What were his dreams?

MOTHER: Modest things . . . He was a modest man.

SON: For instance?

MOTHER: A new suit . . . He felt like a king when he was elegantly dressed . . . Money for the opera . . . a vacation . . .

SON: Did you ever go on a vacation?

MOTHER: Never. And for all those reasons . . . he was angry, bitter . . . . and he became mean.

SON: How mean?

MOTHER: He felt the need to . . . torture someone.

SON (*surprised and alarmed*): "Torture?"

MOTHER *(correcting herself, softening the sentence)*: Psychologically. Only psychologically. He felt the need to make you suffer, to humiliate you. He had that need to feel alive, superior, a real macho.

SON *(surprised and upset)*: That surprises me. I never thought he was like that . . .

MOTHER *(with curiosity, she's trying to understand)*: Have you ever wanted to make someone suffer? One of your girl friends?

SON: Suffer how?

MOTHER: Tormenting her, joking with malice.

SON: Who should I torment?

MOTHER: A sister, your lovers.

SON: No, no. Absolutely no.

MOTHER *(with sadness)*: He, on the contrary, he never missed a chance to humiliate me. You, did you ever feel the desire to humiliate your women?

SON: Never! We are equal. Our generation has finally accepted the principle of equality. We give and take, both of us. On the same level.

MOTHER: To give, to take, they are two vulgar verbs. Merchants use them. You, men, what do you give?

SON *(slightly ironically)*: "Love" . . .

MOTHER: "Love?"

SON *(still mocking)*: You read it in that magazine. Man gives "love" to have sex. Women give "sex" to have love.

MOTHER: You see? Poor women! They are making a sacrifice to obtain . . .

SON: You still have this medieval concept of sacrifice. We are equal! We desire! They desire! Them too! They are not making a sacrifice! They are like us! Absolute equality!

MOTHER: It's men who always get more out of it.

SON: It's false! Absolutely false! You don't know this, Mother. And I can't explain it to you.

MOTHER: Why not?

SON: It's too complicated. We're living in a new world. In a difficult world.

MOTHER: Tell me about it.

SON *(with some difficulty)*: Modern women, the feminists – and they're all feminists today – they know what they want, they know their rights.

MOTHER: Rights? It seems fair to me . . .

SON: And they often get much more . . . *(he hesitates)* . . . of what we get.

MOTHER: What do you mean? You are together. Two souls that become one. Two halves of a couple of lovers. They complete each other. Two, a couple, equal.

SON: You see? You don't understand. In a couple, one of the two always gets more.

MOTHER: That's absurd! Even if it were true – once you enjoy it more, another time she will enjoy it more. What's wrong with that?

SON *(uneasy)*: Mother, where do you find such verbs?

MOTHER *(ironically)*: In the dictionary, I enjoy an ice-cream, a walk, a . . .

SON *(interrupting)*: That's enough! That's enough!

MOTHER *(smiling)*: I was about to say, a swim. You know, I like swimming. *(A brief pause.)* You men hold the keys of the world. Fathers, brothers, teachers, priests, doctors. And you charm many women with your power. I was fascinated by his power. The power to love, caress, protect, heal, placate my anguish as a woman. *(The son stares at her, studies her.)*

That was my mistake, maybe. To believe that he really had all that power.

SON: Men had that power. Dad too, maybe. You have a different one, the right one. The instinct for being sweet and good.

MOTHER: They taught us that to conquer a man, to gain his approval, we had to be "docile" . . . *(she corrects herself)* sweet and passive.

SON: It helps, in a relationship.

MOTHER: They taught us that a man is the head of the family, the protector, the replica and image of our Lord, the "Lord" of one's life.

SON: Not all of us. We are different. We don't think like that any longer. I think I'm different from Dad.

MOTHER *(staring at him)*: You are.

SON: What do you see in me that reminds you of him? What do we have in common?

MOTHER: Nothing.

SON: You see? You understand, you sense intelligent women take everything with a grain of salt. The husband, the father, is not the "master." He is a companion, a friend. You are intelligent. You should have seen it, you should have understood it.

MOTHER: I know it today. Too late, maybe.

SON: It's never too late. You are relatively young . . .

MOTHER: "Relatively?"

SON: Sixty is not so —

MOTHER: Fifty-nine.

SON: Did you feel loved by Dad?

MOTHER *(reflecting)*: I thought, I felt . . . I had that impression. I only wanted his approval.

SON: What kind of approval?

MOTHER: To be accepted, praised, to have the confirmation that he felt my presence at his side, that I was his woman. And the more absent-minded, detached, aloof, he was the more I struggled for his approval.

SON: He had a difficult life, full of worries. Not all men have the time to give constant approval. They have a hundred things to do. This life is a continuous struggle. One has no time to repeat "I love you, I love you, *ad infinitum.*" One even becomes ridiculous.

MOTHER: He who confirms, consoles, worships, is never ridiculous. (*A pause. The son looks at his mother with tears in his eyes; she's a wonderful woman.*)

SON: Did he ever show he was weak?

MOTHER: In a certain sense, he was . . . strong. On other occasions, he was not.

SON: He was human, you see? Sometimes strong, sometimes weak.

MOTHER: Human.

SON: What do you mean by strong?

MOTHER: He always felt this need to give orders. He always had to have the last word. He left us.

SON: What do you mean by weak?

MOTHER: He liked to give orders. That's a sign of weakness. He always had to have the last word. That's a sign of weakness. He left us. Only a weak man abandons his family.

SON: You never told me how, why. What happened that last day?

MOTHER: There are things that do not seem real if you don't talk about them. I never speak about my mother's death. Never. She's therefore alive in me, the way I saw her that last time. I never speak about that last day with him. It is as if it never happened.

SON *(with curiosity)*: Did anything special happen? A quarrel, some vague accusation?

MOTHER: No. He left through that door. Maybe he will reappear at any moment.

(They stare at the door as if they were waiting.)

SON *(after a short silence; changing subject)*: Was he jealous of Rosanna's boyfriends?

MOTHER *(vague)*: Yes, sure . . . it's human to defend, to protect . . .

SON: Protect her from what?

MOTHER: He was afraid they would take her away from him, maybe . . . that they would "use" her, as he used to say. *(She stares at the son who is avoiding her look. He thinks like that too.)*

SON: He loved her. He wanted to protect her.

MOTHER: Yes.

SON *(cautiously)*: Going away, therefore, ceasing to protect . . . means that he didn't love her . . .

MOTHER *(struck by this statement, looking at him questioningly)*: He left me. Therefore he didn't love me.

SON: You were too human, too weak.

(A silence; the telephone rings; the mother comes back to reality; she picks up the receiver.)

MOTHER: Yes . . . *(she listens carefully, alarmed)* Where? Where is she now? *(The son is now interested in what is happening.)* All right . . . Thank you . . . *(hangs up).*

SON: What happened?

MOTHER: Rosanna . . .

SON: What happened to her?

MOTHER: She had an accident.
SON: Again?
MOTHER: She's at the hospital. We have to go.
SON (*irritated, nervously*): Why? Why must we always
run to help her, to get her out of the trouble she
gets herself in?
MOTHER: Because we love her.
(*She exits, almost running. The son moves slowly, reluc-
tantly.*)

Curtain

ACT TWO

The daughter is in a wheelchair, she has a black eye and other wounds. One leg is in a cast. She is listening to pop music, feeling it and following it with body movement. The mother stares at her while she is knitting.

MOTHER *(after a long silence, when the music stops)*: He called.

DAUGHTER *(surprised)*: Who? The bastard who did this to me? Where did he find my phone number?

MOTHER: No . . . He called . . . He . . .

DAUGHTER: He who?

MOTHER: You know very well . . .

DAUGHTER *(nervous, angry)*: No. Tell me. Who?

MOTHER *(after a short hesitation)*: Your first love.

DAUGHTER *(with irritation)*: What did he want?

MOTHER: He must have known that . . .

DAUGHTER: What did he want?

MOTHER: He asked about you. How you are feeling? If you needed anything? Do you need anything?

DAUGHTER: No.

MOTHER: He was very worried, really. He offered any kind of help. He made me understand that he is offering money too.

DAUGHTER: We don't need it.

MOTHER: He would like to . . . *(she hesitates)*.

DAUGHTER *(ironically)*: What would he like?

MOTHER: To see us again.

DAUGHTER: No!

MOTHER: It's high time that you forgave him. Your life is not . . .

DAUGHTER *(interrupting)*: My life is mine, the way I want it! It's all mine!

MOTHER *(cautiously)*: It's not fair. You should face the situation and . . .

DAUGHTER: I said no. It's no! The chapter is closed. Over and done with.

MOTHER: It's not fair that your . . .

DAUGHTER *(interrupting)*: Change the subject. You know me. I never change my mind.

MOTHER: You are pitiless.

DAUGHTER *(proud of it)*: I am pitiless, yes!

MOTHER: It was always your shortcoming. What do you have where your heart should be? A piece of steel?

DAUGHTER: It has become steel. Yes. Become. It's their fault. One is worse than the other.

MOTHER: Maybe it's a little bit your fault too.

DAUGHTER: Oh yes! That's how you defend your daughter? My fault?

MOTHER: One must be flexible, human.

DAUGHTER: Human? You think I'm not human? Look at these wounds! I break! I am made of flesh! I am painfully vulnerable. More than you who have learned never to cry!

MOTHER *(ignoring)*: No more waiting. No more of your ambiguous stalling. It's much better if he knows.

DAUGHTER: Know what?

MOTHER: Everything. You cannot keep a secret like this all your life.

DAUGHTER: I said no and it's *no*! You swore it, you remember? We swore together, on Daddy's grave!

MOTHER (*alarmed; she hopes he is still alive*): What grave? Where? You know something? What happened? When? Where?

DAUGHTER: Calm down. I don't know anything. Don't you remember? You chose that word. "Grave." When he left us, you decided he was dead to all of us.

MOTHER: It's not true.

DAUGHTER: Very true! You said it. I remember perfectly: "I swear on his grave that this will be our secret forever. We'll never tell anyone!" You agreed with me. Full agreement.

MOTHER: I never thought he was . . . dead. If he came back tomorrow . . .

DAUGHTER: Would you forgive him? Would you let him join our family again?

MOTHER: Certainly. If you really love someone you can forgive.

DAUGHTER: Only the weak forgive. Betrayal cannot be forgiven. Must not be forgiven.

MOTHER (*with hope*): Oh no! If he came back . . .

DAUGHTER: You were always weak. With him, with me, with Carlo.

MOTHER: With you too?

DAUGHTER: With me too.

MOTHER: You see? You cannot be human and tolerant. You're reproaching me now. What should I have done? Kicked you out of the house? Not accept your way of life? I wouldn't have been able to. You are too strong for me. And look at the irony of the whole thing. I have lost the man I loved because I was too weak, maybe. You . . . because you're too strong, aggressive, exuberant.

DAUGHTER: I wasn't like that. I've become like that.

MOTHER: Oh no! Since you were a child, you were strong, stubborn, obstinate! Like now, for instance. Why don't you give him another chance? He repented, he's always calling, he's begging us to . . .

DAUGHTER: The chapter is closed.

MOTHER: And with Carlo, you're so stubborn with him too. You should help him.

DAUGHTER: Help him?

MOTHER: Truth helps. It gives new perspectives, it creates new feelings. It's time you told him the truth. That's enough with your lies. They are hurting you, they are hurting all of us.

(The son comes in. He obviously heard her last words.)

SON *(repeating)*: That's enough with your lies! Sounds like a good idea! What lies are you talking about? *(The mother exits in silence. She ignores him. She prefers to leave them alone.)*

SON *(sitting near Rosanna)*: How are you feeling?

DAUGHTER: I'm all right.

SON: It's your best quality.

DAUGHTER: Which one?

SON: Even if you are in a thousand pieces, you'll always say "I'm all right."

DAUGHTER: It's the truth. I feel okay.

SON: It's the only quality of yours I admire.

DAUGHTER *(ironically)*: The only one?

SON: The most important, the most real. You are a strong woman, proud and stubborn. *(After a brief silence.)* What kind of lies was she talking about?

It's not true that you were with your friend Anita? What truth should you reveal to me?

DAUGHTER *(staring at him, exploding)*: That I hate all men!

SON *(calm, taking her hand)*: I know that. And I also know that you don't feel too well. You seem restless.

DAUGHTER: With a leg like this? Who wouldn't be? I can't go wherever I want to go. I'm nailed here!

SON: That's better. It gives you a chance to rest a little.

DAUGHTER: I don't need rest! I have a thousand things to do!

SON: Mother is taking care of them.

DAUGHTER: I don't mean here. I mean in my office. Outside!

SON: They'll survive without you. You're not . . .

DAUGHTER: . . . indispensable! I am! Without me, it's a mess!

(A short silence. The son does not like her attitude.)

SON *(ignoring her)*: You must learn to calm down, to accept life the way it is.

DAUGHTER: Oh yes, of course! Take it as it comes. And when it comes it falls like a ton of bricks on my head! I need to get out, to go, to fly away!

SON: The usual crazy desire for independence.

DAUGHTER: That's it! I don't want to depend on any man! I want to be alone, on my own two feet, without anybody's help! That's the way I want to live and die! Independent! *(A silence.)*

SON: What was Mother talking about? She said, "It's enough with your lies, tell the truth." What truth?

DAUGHTER *(exploding)*: That I hate men, I told you! All of them. You know that.

SON: All of them? Me too?

DAUGHTER (*caressing his hair*): Not you. (*She looks at him with love.*) You are . . . (*Hesitates.*)

SON: . . . Your sweet little brother. You called me "love," I remember that. You used to hug me, kiss me.

DAUGHTER: You were adorable.

SON: And now?

DAUGHTER: You are a big tough boy. Ugly and selfish like everybody else.

SON: How do you know that?

DAUGHTER: All men are selfish.

SON: How many did you know? Two, three? Are you sure we're all so terrible? (*Inquisitively.*) How many?

DAUGHTER (*avoiding him*): Too many. All the same.

SON: How many?

DAUGHTER: I'll never tell you. You're the jealous type, like . . . (*She hesitates.*)

SON: Like?

DAUGHTER: Like Daddy. He never let me out of the house.

SON: He did the right thing. The three men you've known, what was wrong with them?

DAUGHTER: You begin to be like Mommy. Inquisitive. She's asking strange questions.

SON: She's asking me too.

DAUGHTER: What does she want to know from you?

SON: Strange, intimate details. What happened? Is she waking up? Is she thinking about dating?

DAUGHTER: It would be high time. What did she ask you?

SON: I thought she was so old fashioned.

DAUGHTER: What did she ask you?

SON: My opinion about you.

DAUGHTER *(surprised)*: About me? What does she want to know? Why doesn't she ask me directly?

SON *(uncertain, he is lying)*: She wants a man's opinion.

DAUGHTER: What opinion? What does she want to know about me?

SON *(cautious, slowly, he is the one who wants to know)*: The reason why you have this need to go out, to take risks.

DAUGHTER: To risk what?

SON: The reasons why you're always looking for new friendships, new chances to quarrel, to take risks.

DAUGHTER: Everyone takes risks all the time. But why is she asking you about these things?

SON: She wants to know if it's chemistry, if it's a biological instinct.

DAUGHTER: In other words, if I am "sick."

SON *(ignoring her)*: Why are you drawn into dangerous situations? You know what men want. You know that, if you say no, they are bound to hurt you. Who is the bastard who beat you up?

DAUGHTER: I don't know, I don't know him. I don't want to know him, to see him again. What else did she ask you?

SON: She began to ask about female desires. The reason why women need a man. She says she never felt that need.

DAUGHTER: Never? Maybe she doesn't know, she doesn't understand it. She misunderstands her pain, her anxiety.

SON: She begins to understand, to guess. She has discovered the word "orgasm."

DAUGHTER *(amused)*: I know. She asked me too. I explained the whole thing.

SON: The whole thing?

DAUGHTER: Why not? She's only sixty.

SON: Fifty-nine.

DAUGHTER *(continuing)*: She's still young.

SON: Wouldn't you be jealous if . . . ?

DAUGHTER: If she found a man? No. She's entitled to live too.

SON: To live. What do you mean by that word?

DAUGHTER: You know. To wake up near a man, in the morning. But I don't think she will ever dare. We arrived at the conclusion that she had only one orgasm in her life. When she conceived me.

SON: And when she conceived me?

DAUGHTER *(correcting herself)*: Oh yes! Of course. When she conceived us. That legend is still alive among women. They all remember "something special, an unusual spark" nine months before their children were born. *(A silence. They study one another.)*

SON: You see, mother asked my opinion from a man's point of view. You, on the contrary . . .

DAUGHTER: Me, on the contrary?

SON: You never ask, you have never asked me . . .

DAUGHTER: What am I supposed to ask?

SON: The opinion of a man, my opinion.

DAUGHTER: You're too young!

SON: You told me once that at fourteen you knew everything, you understood everything. So did I.

DAUGHTER: Men are slower, more immature.

SON: By a couple of years they say . . . At sixteen, therefore, I knew everything.

DAUGHTER: Everything about what?

SON: Life, love, women.

DAUGHTER (*ironically*): So young! You think like Daddy.

SON: Not exactly at sixteen, but more or less . . .

DAUGHTER: What do you know about women?

SON: A great deal. But this is not the important thing. An intelligent woman like you wouldn't make so many mistakes if . . .

DAUGHTER: So many mistakes if . . . ?

SON: I don't mean you alone. Other women too. They should ask their fathers, their brothers, a trusted friend, how we think.

DAUGHTER: Tell me, how do you think?

SON: To communicate is important, very important. You never tried to talk, open up . . .

DAUGHTER: Because in you, I always saw a child, a beardless young boy. (*Carlo caresses his face.*) You are almost twenty years younger than me.

SON: Even at my age one knows a great deal.

DAUGHTER: I know, I know that you are smart, intelligent and inquisitive. Maybe we never had time to communicate because we are a family. One never speaks in a family.

SON: That's a big mistake.

DAUGHTER: Let's begin today. I'm stuck here, I have nothing else to do. Let's talk. What do you want to tell me? Obvious things?

SON: That's why people never talk in a family. Because they think they know everything about everybody. They think they can guess what the other ones, mother, wife, husband, brother are about to say.

DAUGHTER: You see how intelligent you are! You're

absolutely right. When Daddy opened his mouth – he hadn't yet uttered a single syllable – I already knew what he was about to say. Same thing with Mommy. *(Studying him.)* Less with you . . . you are aloof, mysterious. I don't always guess what you're about to say . . . Let me guess *(stares at him; studies him)* Are you in love?

SON: No.

DAUGHTER: Even if you're not in love you want to marry her all the same?

SON: No.

DAUGHTER: You want to run away from this crazy family?

SON: I want to stay here and improve it. I want to improve our relationship. Mother deserves it. *(A brief pause.)* You deserve it. You too.

DAUGHTER *(vaguely ironic)*: Thank you! Surprise me. What can you do for both of us? Two women alone, two desperate women.

SON: It's not true. Mother is serene. You could become serene.

DAUGHTER: I could . . . When? How?

SON: If you are ready to listen to a man's opinion.

DAUGHTER *(slightly ironic)*: A real man. All right. Tell me everything.

SON: Mother asked me why I don't understand women. She made me think about it. It's true. It's difficult to understand a woman.

DAUGHTER: And men are easy to understand?

SON: I'm ready to admit that it's difficult, very difficult to understand a man too.

DAUGHTER: How true!

SON: Unless a husband, a boyfriend, a brother, opens up and confesses himself, revealing his feelings.

DAUGHTER: Speak, little brother, and surprise me.

SON: You see? You're always ironic. And you always like to joke! I'm serious. I want to explain how we are, our nature, what we think, what we want.

DAUGHTER: Enough with joking. I'm all ears. Honestly. (*Looks at him with love.*) And I want to tell you today that I love you very much. I feel I love you very very much. You're adorable, like before, like always, when I had more time for you.

SON (*moved*): Me too. I've always been in love with you, full of admiration for your energy, your strength, your intelligence.

DAUGHTER (*happy and vaguely ironic*): How many compliments from my love today! (*She takes his head and gives him a quick peck on his lips.*) Tell me, naughty boy. What do you tell your women before you . . . do those things to them? What's your secret, your "method?"

SON (*serious*): All right. Let's start with the word "method." It's a false concept, it's the wrong idea. Men don't follow a method.

DAUGHTER: They all have a way of behaving, a special way to convince, to conquer.

SON: There is no method.

DAUGHTER: All right. This is new to me, but . . . (*encouraging him*) . . . I knew that my little brother knew how to be original. Keep talking. Elaborate.

SON: Without being aware of it, it's our nature, it's a biological instinct, each of us, when he sees a beautiful woman, he wants to procreate.

DAUGHTER (*surprised*): Procreate?

SON: To make a baby.

DAUGHTER: I know what it means. But you've got to be kidding.

SON: In theory. I mean that, without being aware of it, we would like our sons, our eternity, our tomorrow to be as beautiful as that woman. The child of a beautiful woman is often very beautiful, the way she is!

DAUGHTER: What about unbeautiful women? Why would a man like to have an unbeautiful child?

SON: That's natural selection. A man who feels less attractive, looks for a woman who is more or less like him, someone who won't reject him.

DAUGHTER (*trying to follow what Carlo is saying*): Therefore any time you've done it with a woman, you wanted to have a baby.

SON: In theory, without being aware of it. One wants to possess a woman who can give us eternity, we want to make love with the wonderful mother of our children!

DAUGHTER: Then why do you all run away after that intimate moment?

SON: A hundred reasons.

DAUGHTER: Tell me five.

SON: Why only five?

DAUGHTER: The most important. We must always look for the essential.

SON: You see? It's mother nature in you. A woman is essential, radical, a real force of mother nature.

DAUGHTER: Thank you for the compliment. Tell me those five reasons.

SON (*looking*): Which ones should I choose among so many?

DAUGHTER: Choose.

SON: Fear. The fear of having a child you must protect in a difficult world like this.

DAUGHTER: First, they all wanted a child! Later, they don't want him any longer! You are real Hamlets, you men! To love or not to love, to give or not to give, to escape today or escape tomorrow! *(Staring at him.)* And after this "fear?"

SON *(reflecting)*: Second reason . . . the realization that she is the wrong woman.

DAUGHTER: Wrong? How can a human being be "wrong?"

SON *(ignoring her)*: There was physical attraction, chemistry, but she did not share his ideas, his way of looking at things.

DAUGHTER: That's a childish excuse. Give them time to grow with you! Third reason.

SON *(searching)*: She's always the same. As you rightly said: "She doesn't grow with you." She's lazy. She just needed to have a man in her life.

DAUGHTER *(ironic)*: That's serious! Fourth reason.

SON: Greed.

DAUGHTER *(surprised)*: Greed? What could she want from you? Your salary is ridiculously small?

SON: Greed is ruling the world today. Either she has too much and wants a man who has as much. Or she has nothing and she looks for someone who has more, as much as possible. The first question is always: "What do you do? Where do you work? How much do you make?"

DAUGHTER: They are human, they want to survive. Fifth reason.

SON: The most serious reason . . . disappointment.

DAUGHTER: Disappointment? What do you want? Acrobatics?

SON: No, we don't want sexual gymnastics.

DAUGHTER: What do you want then?

SON: Precisely the opposite of such games, but . . .

DAUGHTER *(interrupting him)*: You mean you don't want sex?

SON: A woman who wants more than sex, one who has more to offer, generously.

DAUGHTER *(studying him with disbelief)*: Incredible!

SON: It seems incredible to you because you never consulted a man who loves you and wants to protect you.

DAUGHTER *(ignoring him)*: According to you, all men want the ignorant little virgin who knows nothing, absolutely nothing *(accusing him)*, so that they can teach her, within their own limitations, of course.

SON: We want a woman who is interested in a man romantically but also a person, as a companion, a woman who knows how to communicate, speak, smile, understand.

DAUGHTER: No sex therefore?

SON: That comes later. We prefer to know her well before. You must first understand each other, admire each other. She must be the companion of your life, a long life.

DAUGHTER *(still unbelieving)*: You, therefore, you didn't make love to your women?

SON: I prefer a woman who says no, who knows how to say no, a woman who knows how to wait. A "virtuous" woman. An old concept which is still valid. Did you ever think that the word virtue comes from *vir,* virility, strength, the wisdom of knowing how to say no?

DAUGHTER *(disbelieving)*: And you, would you tell things like this to your women?

SON: Oh no! These are secrets, things you only tell your sister, your daughter.

DAUGHTER: Obviously! Mothers, sisters and daughters are not to be touched. They are sacred! *(To him directly, staring.)* But we are all someone's mother, sister and daughter!

SON: You see, Rosanna *(it's the first time he's calling her by name),* nature pushes us to possess, enjoy, generate, but after making love there is disappointment, regret. *Post coitum, fletum,* the Latins used to say. "After copulation, tears."

DAUGHTER: I realize now I made a mistake to make you study with the priests.

SON *(surprised)*: You? You are the one who chose that school for me?

DAUGHTER *(correcting herself)*: Mommy. Dad, me. A family decision. It's not the first time that I've heard that kind of preaching. And you know by whom? The answer is obvious. You know by whom?

SON: By whom?

DAUGHTER: By Dad. You and Dad, you think the same way. Only men who are jealous speak like that . . . *(Staring at him.)* Are you jealous of me? Of my life?

(The mother enters with a beautiful bunch of flowers. She leaves the door open. Behind her, offstage, we see a bright light. She approaches her daughter in silence and puts the flowers near her. She indicates an envelope which is visible

among the flowers. The daughter ignores it. The mother takes the envelope and places it in her hands. The mother exits without uttering a word. A silence. The daughter puts down the envelope. She ignores it.)

SON: Aren't you curious?

DAUGHTER: No.

SON: Who sent those flowers? The bastard who beat you up?

DAUGHTER: No. He is not the type who sends flowers.

SON: Who is it then?

DAUGHTER: I don't care.

SON: Maybe you know. I'm sure you know.

DAUGHTER *(ignoring)*: We were talking about jealousy before. Are you jealous? Have you ever sent flowers like those to a woman you have betrayed?

SON: Then it's the one who betrayed you. Who is he?

DAUGHTER: Why are you so jealous? Of Mommy too, I bet. Think for a moment. If Mommy, your mother, were in bed with someone, what would you think? Would you be jealous?

SON *(reflecting)*: No. But I prefer not to think about it. Mothers are above it all . . . they don't do . . .

DAUGHTER: . . . those things. You really are a child. Before you were talking about a biological instinct in you men. Physical attraction, chemistry, as you defined it. Well, that attraction, that desire, well, mothers have it too! All the women in this world. We are incomplete without a family.

SON: Without a man, you mean.

DAUGHTER: Without a companion.

SON: Anyone, one after the other?

DAUGHTER: You know what every woman's dream

is? To meet a great love, at sixteen. To adore him, to be adored. A serene, quiet, happy life with him. Forever! But men betray you, at sixteen, at twenty, at thirty. They always betray you. One after the other. That's why we are always looking for that vanishing dream!

SON: If you learned how to say "no," to wait . . .

DAUGHTER: Try to say "no." *(Shows her wounds.)* They torture you!

SON: Maybe you sent false signals, the hint of a promise, an invitation to . . .

DAUGHTER *(angry)*: Change the subject! It's what the cops say, after cases like these. I don't want to hear that from your lips!

SON *(apologetic)*: Forgive me, I only meant . . .

DAUGHTER: You know what we want, we women? Mommy mentioned it one day. A strange sentence that struck me, and I have never forgotten. She said, "I would like a man as kind to me as a sister." Mommy had a sister she adored . . .

(The mother comes in again. She leaves the door open behind her. A bright light from offstage. She advances toward the daughter decidedly. She takes the envelope. She opens it. She gives a letter to her the daughter. She withholds a check.)

MOTHER: Read! He is sorry about everything, he still loves you, he wants to marry you. *(She shows the check.)* He is rich now. This money is for the first expenses, in your own home.

(The daughter tears the letter without reading it. The mother was about to hand her the check, withholds it, fearing she may tear that too.)

SON *(looking in the direction of the open door, of the bright *light which perhaps signifies a luminous future)*: But who is this man who insists so much and is offering so much?

MOTHER *(handing him the check)*: Ask her.

SON *(to his sister, insisting)*: Who is he?

    (A long silence.)

DAUGHTER *(staring at him)*: I was sixteen, he was twenty-one . . . a great passion . . . he left me, he disappeared. He is your father. I hate him. He destroyed all my dreams. He has poisoned me, betrayed me. Do you want him? Do you want to accept him in our "family?" He is rich. *(The son finally looks at the check. There is a reaction. It must be a large amount.)* It would solve all our problems, and after all, you said that greed rules the world today. *(A brief pause. She studies him.)* Do you want him? Do you want him in my bed? Do you want me to say yes?

    (The mother stares at the son with hope. The son slowly approaches Rosanna, his new mother. He kneels down beside her. He looks at her, with love.)

SON: No . . . *(He tears the check)* No . . . We don't need anyone . . .

    (A warm embrace. The mother is petrified, disappointed. She would have been able to forgive. Immobility. A tableau.)

The End

LOVERS

Characters

Eugene: a handsome distinguished-looking man.
Marisa: a beautiful woman in her late twenties.
Tess: Marisa's friend.
Ursula: a true amazon; tall, robust, imposing. A detective.

Time and place: New York today.

ACT ONE

The living room of an elegant New York apartment. A couch, armchairs, coffee table, phone, liquor cabinet and paintings on the walls. Eugene arrives home, obviously tired. He sits heavily on the couch and takes off his shoes.

EUGENE: Marisa! I'm home. (*No answer.*) Marisa! (*Marisa enters looking calm and serene. She walks slowly to the couch, gazes at her husband, then sits down at a good distance from him.*)

EUGENE: It's been a hell of a day. That idiot, Schutzman, is still giving me a hard time. Any suggestion from me . . . any idea is dismissed with contempt, as if I were some imbecile. One of these days I may strangle him. What a bunch of neurotics! Useless people . . . afraid of anything new — afraid of everything! No experimenting for them. They all go in their own shells, frightened, myopic . . . No one communicates anymore . . . How are you today?

MARISA: Fine.

EUGENE: You know what I do lately? Whenever anyone asks me how I am, I say I have a bad headache. They go right on talking, as if I'd said "Well, thank you." They don't hear, they don't even listen. We're living in a world of little islands, a world of failures and alienation. Where's the mail?

MARISA: (*points to a small table near the front door*) Where it always is.

(Eugene is a bit surprised by his wife's manner. He gets up and gets the mail, returns to his seat and opens a few letters.)

EUGENE: Bills. "Please donate." "Please renew your subscription." How about a drink, please?

MARISA *(pointing to the liquor cabinet)*: The glasses are over there.

(Eugene looks at her in surprise. This is unusual behavior for his wife. He gets up and prepares his drink.)

EUGENE: You seem low this evening. Nervous. Has something happened?

MARISA: No.

EUGENE: You seem strange, tense. Are you okay?

MARISA: I'm okay.

EUGENE: I'm a bit tired, but if you want, we could go to a movie tonight.

MARISA: No.

EUGENE: There's Woody Allen's latest movie.

MARISA: I've seen it.

EUGENE: Oh, good. Did you go alone? With your sister?

MARISA: Alone.

EUGENE: Do you want to eat out tonight?

MARISA: No.

EUGENE *(sits down again and studies her, holds out his feet)*: Please, get me my slippers.

MARISA: You know where they are.

EUGENE *(gets up, ready to get his slippers himself, ironic)*: Sorry! You are so antagonistic today. You usually love to pamper me.

MARISA *(sarcastically)*: "Pamper?"

EUGENE: That was my impression, at least. I'll get my slippers. Then let's talk.

(Eugene exits. Marisa swallows his drink, perhaps to give herself courage. She makes a face; she doesn't like alcohol. Eugene re-enters with his slippers on, sits down, and observes Marisa.)

EUGENE: Tell me, darling, what happened today? Whom did you see today?

MARISA: No one.

EUGENE: Did you speak to your mother?

MARISA: No.

(Eugene picks up his glass to drink, sees that it is empty, and is surprised and puzzled.)

EUGENE: You see what happens when I'm worried? I thought the glass was full. I could have sworn . . . You don't drink . . . so I must be confused. You see the effect you have on me? *(Goes to refill his glass.)* Now tell me everything. Did you fight with somebody?

MARISA: No.

EUGENE: You burnt dinner. All right, so what?

MARISA: I didn't cook.

EUGENE *(attempts to caress her. Marisa avoids him.)* Tell me what's wrong, please. I'm your husband, your best friend.

MARISA *(with irony)*: Ah!

EUGENE: All right. You don't consider me your best friend, I'm just your husband. Trust me. Tell me.

MARISA: I have nothing to say. I'm tired of being your servant.

EUGENE *(patiently)*: Let's discuss it. I've offered many times to get you a maid. You always refused.

MARISA: I'm tired of this life.

EUGENE: Understandable . . . Human . . . This is a

tiring, exhausting city. I can take some time off. We could go to Europe.

MARISA: No.

EUGENE: South America.

MARISA: No.

EUGENE: Where do you want to go? Pick a place.

MARISA: Not with you.

EUGENE: If you want to go alone, if you prefer . . . it's all right but why are you so angry?

MARISA: A hundred reasons.

EUGENE: Give me three.

MARISA (*firmly and decisively*): You're selfish. You're boring. I don't love you anymore.

EUGENE (*after a short silence*): Cruel. Below the belt. What can I do to make you happy again?

MARISA: Nothing.

EUGENE: "Nothing" is impossible, my dear. Let's just go over this, point by point, blow by blow. "Selfish," you said. Perhaps it's true. We're all a bit selfish. If I spent more time with you, maybe . . .

MARISA: It wouldn't change a thing.

EUGENE: "Boring." If we spent more time together . . . Do you remember when we were engaged? We went to museums, concerts, we took trips, always laughing . . . We were happy.

MARISA: "Were."

EUGENE (*reflecting*): You no longer love me. I still love you. I always do my best to make you happy. You know what I mean.

MARISA: Gymnastics in bed don't help. You know I don't feel anything. I never have with you.

EUGENE (*trying to ignore the implication*): Now don't

exaggerate. There are times when you have shown signs of pleasure. You react.

MARISA: Act, not react.

EUGENE (*after a short pause*): I'm sorry. Maybe there's a physical problem that you should . . .

MARISA (*interrupting*): It's your problem. Not mine.

EUGENE (*patiently*): Perhaps. All things are possible. We could both go for counseling.

MARISA: No need of that for me.

EUGENE: Good for you, but what makes you so sure?

MARISA: I know. (*Stares at him, defiant.*) I know what pleasure feels like.

EUGENE: How do you know? If you feel something when . . . it means . . . (*Silence. Wanting to avoid a direct confrontation.*) What do you suggest?

MARISA: Divorce. Find yourself another place to live.

EUGENE: This place belongs to me too. I invested . . .

MARISA: My father put it in my name. Wisely. It's mine.

EUGENE: Let's be reasonable. You're upset, unusually so. Go away somewhere, alone, or with me, or with your family. We'll talk about this again when you get back in a few days, in a month, two months. Stay away as long as you want.

MARISA: I've made up my mind. We're through. (*Silence.*)

EUGENE (*cautiously*): You hinted that with me, you feel nothing.

MARISA: I said it clearly. Nothing.

EUGENE: At the same time, you are sure you don't have sexual problems . . . Therefore with someone else . . .

MARISA: Exactly.

EUGENE: You have a lover?

MARISA (*after a brief hesitation, looking at him defiantly*): Yes.

EUGENE: Since when?

MARISA: A few months. I'm happy. I feel alive, at last.

EUGENE: Do I know him?

MARISA: No.

EUGENE: Where's he from? Where do you meet him?

MARISA: Here in town.

EUGENE: Where?

MARISA: Not far from here.

EUGENE: So, while I'm at work . . .

MARISA (*defiantly*): I've found happiness. These things happen. Accept it.

EUGENE: That's not so easy. I still love you.

MARISA: Nothing lasts forever.

EUGENE: At least I have the right to know who he is.

MARISA: You'll know.

EUGENE: I won't go like this, sneaking out like a thief, like an unsatisfactory servant, fired on the spot. I want to know if he's good enough for you, if he'll really make you happy.

MARISA: There's no doubt about that.

EUGENE: Who is he? Where does he live?

MARISA (*after a brief hesitation*): In this building.

EUGENE (*surprised*): Here! Then I must know him.

MARISA: By sight.

EUGENE: Let's see . . . tall, short, old?

MARISA: My age.

EUGENE: Young and strong then. The doctor on the 14th floor?

MARISA: No.

EUGENE: The lawyer with the skimpy blond beard?

MARISA: No.

EUGENE: The unemployed actor with a different girl-
friend every week?

MARISA: No.

EUGENE: Marisa, I love you. I have an obligation to
take care of you. I'm not leaving this house until
you tell me who he is.

MARISA *(reflects)*: If I call and this person comes here,
will you behave?

EUGENE: I promise.

MARISA: No scenes?

EUGENE: Absolutely not.

MARISA: Then you'll go to a hotel, somewhere. I'll
write you out a check. I can be generous, you know.

EUGENE *(with slight irony)*: Yes, I can see you've been
very generous . . .

MARISA: You promise then? I'll introduce you. You'll
behave. And then you'll leave the two of us here,
alone.

EUGENE: In my home?

MARISA: My home. You know that.

EUGENE: In my bed?

MARISA: My father paid for everything in this house,
including the bed.

EUGENE: I shouldn't have let that happen, and now
it's too late. My only consolation will be . . . This
is not my house. This is not my bed.

MARISA: Shall I call?

EUGENE: Call.

(*While Marisa is on the phone, Eugene goes into the
bedroom to put his shoes on again.*)

MARISA *(on the phone)*: Everything's going well. I've

spoken to him. He knows everything. Come down-stairs.

(*Eugene comes back, sits on the couch, and ties his shoelaces.*)

MARISA (*still on the phone*) All right. Don't worry. He's here with me. He's waiting to meet you. Use the key. We're in the living room. (*Hangs up.*)

EUGENE: The key? So it's really true that husbands are the last to know. I must say I never expected this from you. Your parents – staunch Republicans and zealous churchgoers – your sister married to a Protestant Minister. (*He makes himself another drink.*) What does your "friend" drink?

MARISA: Scotch. Straight.

EUGENE: Well, perfect hospitality in this house. I'll fix it myself. (*Returns to the table with two glasses.*) Do you want a drink too to celebrate this rare event?

MARISA: You know I never drink.

EUGENE: I can't believe this. Am I dreaming? Is this really happening to me?

MARISA: It's true. You have always told me that one must know how to face reality.

EUGENE: And now the pupil cheerfully teaches the teacher.

MARISA: No longer a pupil, but a woman, new, free, happy. That's always been your problem, seeing me as a child.

EUGENE (*applauding lightly and mockingly*): Congratu-lations!

(*Sound of a key in the lock. Silence. Muted footsteps.*

Silence. Enter Tess, a beautiful woman. Eugene is startled.)

EUGENE *(stands up and with a slight bow)*: This is obviously a joke.

MARISA & TESS *(together)*: Tess.

EUGENE: A beautiful name. We've smiled at each other in the elevator. You have a lot of "visitors," I noticed.

TESS: I'm an interior decorator. I have many friends.

EUGENE: Please sit down. And I took the liberty of fixing you a drink.

TESS *(sits and takes the glass)*: Thank you. *(Raises the glass.)*

EUGENE *(does the same)*: To Marisa's good health.

TESS: To Marisa.

(They drink. There is a brief silence.)

EUGENE: Among your friends, there's that tall, bald black man.

TESS: Yes, Jeffrey. Marisa knows him.

EUGENE: So you are the one who has been affecting all this change in Marisa. Her new defiance.

TESS: I don't find her defiant. Marisa is shy and reserved. She likes to stay home. I prefer her that way. Much more my type.

EUGENE *(slowly, carefully)*: Your type? What does that mean?

TESS: Marisa told me on the phone that you know everything.

EUGENE *(wary)*: She told me some story . . . strange, vague . . .

TESS: It's not a story.

EUGENE *(continuing)*: According to Marisa, she's taken a passionate lover who lives in this building.

TESS *(to Marisa)*: Thank you. *(Marisa smiles at her.)*

EUGENE: Thanks for what?

TESS: For that . . . "passionate."

EUGENE: Do you mean to tell me that . . . You want me to believe that you . . . *(to Tess)* . . . in spite of your many boyfriends . . .

TESS: Only friends. Love, I've found here.

EUGENE *(incredulously, to Marisa)*: She's the one who makes you happy?

MARISA: Tess is the one.

EUGENE: She gives you more happiness than what I . . . ?

MARISA: She does.

EUGENE *(reflectively)* Spiritually, perhaps . . . friends, sisters . . .

MARISA: Lovers.

EUGENE *(still unbelieving, slowly)*: She, that woman, is better than me?

MARISA: She is.

EUGENE: Knows more than me?

MARISA *(caustically)*: It doesn't take much.

EUGENE *(hurt)*: Thanks again. *(There is a silence as he thinks.)* You know, I'm realistic, I listen, and evaluate . . . I accept what you tell me as possibly true. I've read somewhere that mechanically, coldly, there can be satisfaction for two women when . . .

MARISA: There is nothing "cold" or "mechanical," as you are hoping. It's much more. Accept it.

EUGENE *(as if to himself)*: Live and learn. She is, then, physically . . .

MARISA: Something I could never have imagined. Something you could never imagine.

EUGENE: Another compliment, thank you. You're

really adorable this evening. *(Still unwilling to yield.)* How is it possible that she, this woman . . . ?

MARISA: Resign yourself, Eugene. It is possible. And now go, and leave us alone. *(Short pause.)* You promised.

EUGENE: I promised before I knew the facts, these facts.

MARISA: What difference does it make? I've decided to begin my life over again with someone else. I've found that someone.

EUGENE *(calmly, choosing his words)*: You mentioned divorce before the entrance of your "princess in shining armor."

TESS *(sarcastically)*: Thanks.

MARISA: Yes, I want a divorce.

EUGENE: If there were another man in your life, one who wanted to marry you and take care of you . . .

MARISA *(interrupting)*: I don't need a man to protect me. We'll be fine together. Our love is protection against the world.

EUGENE: There's the hostility of society. Not everyone will understand or be tolerant . . .

MARISA *(taking Tess's hand)*: We're not afraid. We can defend ourselves.

EUGENE *(quietly and slowly)*: You can't marry, of course.

TESS: Yes, we can. It wouldn't be the first time. If Marisa is willing . . .

MARISA: It's not necessary.

EUGENE: Fine. We agree at least on this particular matter. Our divorce is not necessary.

MARISA: Give up, Eugene. I've made up my mind. It's

over. Let me know where you're staying. My lawyer
will get in touch with you.

EUGENE *(calmly and slowly)*: I'm staying here. *(Silence.
The two women look at each other questioningly.)* But
don't worry. I accept the reality of the situation.

TESS: Which means?

MARISA: What are you saying?

EUGENE: I accept this happening . . . this . . . love.

MARISA: Explain.

EUGENE *(carefully, slowly)*: It's not the first time that
a husband finds out and accepts because he loves
his wife.

MARISA *(scornfully)* What love? It's over between us.

EUGENE: I still love you. I'll make any sacrifice to keep
this love alive.

MARISA: Make the sacrifice of leaving. Get out.

TESS: Let him talk. He has something up his sleeve.
What do you propose?

EUGENE: Very simple. I love my wife. I'll permit her
to see you.

TESS *(derisively)*: How generous!

MARISA: I certainly don't need your permission.

TESS: We'd be forced to meet like thieves, as if we were
stealing something that already belongs to us.

EUGENE *(very calmly)*: No . . . you could see each other
whenever and wherever you want.

TESS *(to Marisa, with sarcasm)*: I had no idea he was so
. . . liberated?

MARISA: He only wants to stay with me for my money.

EUGENE: You know very well that your father put
everything in your name. I only have my salary.
That's enough for me.

MARISA *(embraces Tess, challenging him)*: I love her. I

want to live with her, go out with her, be proud of
  her and of our love. For everyone to see.
EUGENE: You can.
MARISA: And you? The unwanted fifth wheel?
EUGENE: Useful third wheel.
MARISA: What do you mean?
TESS: Let him go on. I want to hear if he's going to say
  what I think he will.
EUGENE *(to Marisa)*: You see? I knew you'd choose an
  intelligent woman. Tess has guessed, she under-
  stands.
MARISA *(to Eugene, confused)*: Understand what?
EUGENE *(slowly, choosing his words)*: Free love: do what
  you want when you want.
MARISA: With you hanging around? No! Your being
  here would poison our relationship.
EUGENE: I can be most discreet.
MARISA: With you in the house, it would be impossi-
  ble for us to be open and real, to be ourselves.
EUGENE: Now it should be easier.
MARISA: Why?
EUGENE: Before, you may have felt guilty about your
  affair. The unavoidable feeling that bothers all the
  unfaithful men or women.
TESS: He seems to know all about it. He must have had
  the experience.
EUGENE *(ignores her and speaks to Marisa)*: You must
  feel relieved now. I know everything and have
  accepted. No more betrayal. *(To Tess.)* What do you
  say, Tess? Do you agree?
TESS *(ignores him. To Marisa)*: He wants something
  more.
MARISA: What more does he want?

TESS: Let him talk. He'll tell you.

MARISA: Why do you want to stay where you're not welcome! What do you want from us?

EUGENE: The main thing, the most important for me is . . . the desire to be near you, to be able to protect you.

MARISA: Protect me from what?

EUGENE: From yourself.

MARISA *(to Tess)*: You see? He hopes to persuade me to leave you.

TESS: He wants something more.

MARISA: I just don't understand you, Tess. What else does he want, in your opinion?

TESS: Ask him where he'd sleep.

MARISA *(to Eugene)*: Where would you sleep?

EUGENE *(vaguely)*: There are lots of beds in this house.

MARISA: Of course you're going to leave your bed . . . *(corrects herself)* . . . my bed to Tess and me.

EUGENE: As I've already explained, I believe in free choice. One sleeps where one wants.

TESS *(to Marisa)*: "Where one wants," you heard?

MARISA: Tess and I want to be together. You, where are you going to sleep?

EUGENE *(still vague)*: Sometimes in the guest room, sometimes in the blue room, sometimes . . .

TESS: He leaves it hanging . . . He wants something more.

EUGENE: Tess understands. She knows the world; she's lived, loved, experimented.

TESS: Just like the typical defeated lover, he's trying to cut me down. Negative picture of me. He's inventing my lurid past to turn you against me.

EUGENE: You're obviously a modern woman, ready for new experiences, sexual, bisexual, tri- . . .

TESS *(breaking in)*: Et cetera, et cetera, *ad infinitum.*

MARISA *(to Eugene)*: What are you trying to do?

EUGENE *(ignoring Marisa, and looking hard at Tess)*: I'm sure that it's not the first time for Tess.

TESS: At his age, he still speaks of the "first time."

EUGENE *(ignoring her)*: If I continue living here, I'll always be on hand, close, available.

TESS: Enter the third wheel. *(To Marisa.)* Now, do you understand?

EUGENE: I don't want to impose on anyone. But I'm an optimist. Some fine day, or afternoon, or night, taken by passion, you might call my name . . .

MARISA: Never!

EUGENE: Never say "never!" I'm sure that Tess has experienced something of the sort. You mustn't underestimate her.

TESS *(nervously, jumping to her feet)*: Of course, he knows all about such things. He's familiar with such experiences!
(She walks slowly to the couch and leans over Eugene from behind.)

TESS *(to Marisa)*: Do you call him Gene or Eugene?

MARISA: I called him Eugene. *(Jeeringly.)* He preferred it that way.

TESS *(quietly and controlled)*: Let's see . . .

EUGENE: Tell me, Tess.

TESS: You don't. . . may I call you Eugene?

MARISA: Of course, Tess. It's the first step.

TESS: You don't know anything about my past, Eugene. Perhaps I've loved once, perhaps more than once. It doesn't matter.

MARISA: It doesn't matter.

TESS (*smiles lovingly at Marisa*): Marisa knows everything about me.

EUGENE: Why don't you bring me up to date? Only fair, isn't it? How many men in your life before. . .? (*Slight gesture toward Marisa.*)

TESS: Maybe none, maybe . . .

EUGENE: There's always a man, the first one, the one who lets you down.

MARISA (*sarcastic*): He, on the other hand, *never* disappointed me!

EUGENE (*hard and flat*): It depends on the bitch. Some of them are alive. (*Marisa goes for him wildly, ready to attack.*)

MARISA: Bastard!

(*Tess comes between them and stops her. Calms her. She whispers without Eugene being aware, but the audience can see her lips moving.*)

TESS: It's not worth it, Marisa . . . (*She motions to indicate that she has an idea.*) Best to keep calm, let's put all our cards on the table.

EUGENE: All our cards.

TESS (*still pacifying Marisa*): I'll tell him everything if he'll do the same.

EUGENE: Great idea, Tess. You begin.

TESS: And then we'll have everything out in the open. You'll tell us clearly and honestly what you have in mind.

EUGENE: I believe in clear and honest. (*Mockingly.*) Marisa does too. She's never lied to me.

TESS: *My* story is simple. Two bad chapters. Marisa knows them. (*Slight hesitation.*) Yes, there was a man in my life, my husband, for three years. Then

I discovered my true nature and I lived with a woman for a few months. Now, I love Marisa. (*She smiles at her lovingly*.)

EUGENE: For how long?

MARISA: Forever.

TESS: Now tell us what you're proposing.

EUGENE: You know.

TESS (*goes to the couch again, behind Eugene*): Tell Marisa. You promised to be clear. What's the ideal solution, in your opinion?

EUGENE: It's obvious, isn't it? I want to stay in this house, which is also mine, my world, with the two of you.

MARISA: We don't want you! You would feel shut out, rejected, ignored!

EUGENE: I'm not at all convinced of that.

MARISA: I've already said it a hundred times! (*Earnestly.*) Eugene, go, I beg of you, go for your own sake.

EUGENE: It's true you've said it many times, but you are the only one who has.

MARISA: Which means?

EUGENE: Tess has a lovely smile. She always smiles at me in the elevator. Tess hasn't even once asked me to leave. Tess is a modern woman. She understood my idea right away, and she's not against it.
(*A short silence.*)

TESS (*to Marisa*): He wants you to believe the impossible. His impossible dream. He wants to sleep with me. He wants to show me that a man . . . (*sneering*) . . . a "real" man like him . . .

MARISA (*Sarcastically*): Ah!

TESS: . . . is what is missing in my life. Right, my dear?

EUGENE: Quite right. I offer myself as third wheel. Three is always more exciting than two! *(Tess starts to strangle Eugene with her leather belt. She tightens it more and more as Eugene struggles desperately.)*

TESS *(to Marisa)*: In my bag! Get it quick!
(Marisa runs to the bag, takes out a gun, and aims it anxiously and fearfully.) Now!
(Eugene is still struggling and seems on the point of freeing himself.) Marisa! Shoot him.
(Marisa takes aim and, obviously unwilling, fires twice. Eugene collapses, fatally wounded. He dies. No one moves.)

Curtain

ACT TWO

An hour later. The body of Eugene has been taken into the bedroom. Marisa is in an armchair, her face in her hands. She is distraught. Tess is cleaning off a tiny bloodstain from the couch where Eugene was shot.

TESS: All done. All's well. The last trace eliminated. (*Silence. She looks at Marisa.*) Marisa, everything's under control, believe me. There's no danger for us, for our love.

MARISA: You promised that you wouldn't, that it wouldn't be necessary . . .

TESS: And you promised to get rid of him in a friendly manner, easily. Did we ever imagine that he would propose joining in to ruin our relationship?

MARISA: I'll never be able to forget this. It was horrible.

TESS: It was necessary. We were forced to do it.

MARISA: But I pulled the trigger. You swore that . . .

TESS: I was ready to do it. The gun was in my bag. I would have done it if . . . Didn't you see how things were going? He was sarcastic, insulting, threatening . . . I had to take the initiative. You helped me, and that's it. (*She approaches Marisa and kisses her gently on the forehead.*) The two of us together. We acted together. Together in everything: action, love, passion.

MARISA: And now? How do we get rid of . . . the body? How can we sleep in that bed?

TESS: Everything calmly. Everything legally.

MARISA (*surprised*): Legally?

TESS: I've told you. A definite plan, bomb-proof, fool-proof.

MARISA (*ironically*): The perfect crime.

TESS: The realization of a perfect love. If we want to protect our love – if we want the best – then we've got to be ready to do anything.

MARISA (*bitterly and sarcastically*): Shall we burn the bed and the body?

TESS: No.

MARISA (*bitterly and as a joke*): The bathtub. We'll dissolve poor Eugene in acid.

TESS: "Poor Eugene."

MARISA: When someone dies . . . poor thing! What will we do? Cut him in little pieces?

TESS: You've read too many detective stories.

MARISA: Never! Not one! And here I am right in the middle of the crucial chapter! My God! My God! (*Crosses herself.*)

TESS (*caressing her*): Get hold of yourself. The plan is well worked out, everything prearranged to the last detail, and it's safe.

MARISA: What do you mean? What's arranged?

TESS: There's someone waiting in my apartment ready to help us.

MARISA: Who is it? You told me you had no other friends. That you live alone. Who's in your apartment? Who did you tell this to? How could you? Why should anyone else help me?

TESS: She'll help both of us.

MARISA: Why take this risk? For what purpose? You told me that only you and I . . . now there's a third person. And who is it? Please don't tell me this! Don't tell me someone else knows about this crime!

TESS: Dial my number. Someone will answer. (*Marisa hesitates.*) Go ahead!
(*Marisa approaches the phone warily, dials slowly. Someone lifts the receiver at the other end. Marisa is startled.*)

MARISA: Who is it? Who's there? Why don't you say something? Hello? Talk, say something! Hello! Hello! Talk!

TESS: Only to me. (*She takes the phone and speaks into it.*) Everything went according to plan. (*Looks at her watch.*) Come here in ten minutes. (*She hangs up. Marisa looks stunned.*)

MARISA: Who's coming up, and why? Is it safe? What are you going to do?

TESS: Calm down. I'll explain everything.

MARISA: Is it one of your lovers?

TESS: I love only you, Marisa. You've got to trust me. I beg you to listen to me. I need your complete trust now. You know I've always told you the truth.

MARISA: Perhaps.

TESS: Don't begin having doubts now. This is the most important moment in our lives, in our relationship. (*Pauses a moment.*) All right then, as I said before, all this will be resolved legally. I wasn't joking, I meant that. This thing can be worked out openly and in the right way. The "law" will help.

MARISA: "The law?" *Who* will help?

TESS: It wouldn't be possible to get rid of that . . . (*gesturing toward the bedroom*) . . . in a sack or wrapped in a rug, or in the tub. That's Agatha Christie. He'll go out of here legally, with the help of the police.

MARISA: Are you crazy?

TESS: No, I'm in love. And fighting for this love. I had to be organized, practical, and precise. The police will be here in a few minutes.

MARISA *(terrified, about to run out)*: Oh no! I'm getting out of here! I can't . . . I'm not . . . *(wringing her hands)* . . . I don't know how to lie! The gun! The fingerprints!

TESS: Everything will be legal, out in the open.

MARISA: In the open? The police? They know everything, they find out everything! I won't go to jail! Not even for a second! I would die!

TESS: Don't worry, I assure you, you won't go to jail!

MARISA: It's easy for you to say that! I'm the one who pulled the trigger! I'm the one who killed him!

TESS: You and I together. And we'll stay together.

MARISA: Together in jail? That's a great comfort!

TESS: Neither of us. Get hold of yourself.

MARISA *(after a short pause)*: Who's coming here? That phone call. Is there really someone in your apartment? Who is it?

TESS: There's only one person: an ally.

MARISA: Do I know this person?

TESS: She's my sister's best friend. A "detective." And she's promised to help us.

MARISA: Oh God! A detective! Why should she help us? Does your sister know about this too? Another one who knows about this! Who else?

TESS: My sister knows nothing about this. This detective owes her a favor, a big favor. She wants to help, and she will.

MARISA: I . . . I can't face her! She's an officer of the law, and she'll know it was me who fired the gun.

TESS: I'll explain everything. You may be right,

though. It might be better if I speak to her alone. Go to the bar there across the street, at the corner. *(Goes to the widow and lifts the curtain. She fixes it so it stays raised and open.)* Keep an eye on this window from the bar. When I lower the curtain again, it will mean that everything is settled, under control. Then you can come back. *(Marisa appears confused and unsure.)* Go now . . . She'll be here any minute. *(Looks at her watch.)* It's really best if I see her alone first. *(She leads Marisa to the door.)* Make sure the doorman sees you downstairs, and that people notice you at the bar. It's part of the plan.

(Marisa obeys passively, following Tess out like an automaton. They exit. There is a short silence, then the sound of footsteps in the hall. Tess and Ursula enter. Ursula is a tall, robust woman, completely self-confident. She has one arm around Tess, protectively. Ursula wears a suit of severe military cut. The bag slung over her shoulder contains a revolver.)

TESS: She might have noticed you.

URSULA: I was curious to see what she's like. A beautiful woman . . . You have good taste.

(They embrace with a certain warmth, controlled. Formerly lovers, there is still some feeling, an attraction remains. Ursula tries to kiss Tess on the mouth, but Tess casually eludes the embrace.)

URSULA *(Lights a cigarette)*: She doesn't resemble me in any way. But you're well-known for your fickleness. You always choose a different type.

TESS: That's all talk. I have loved only you, and now . . .

URSULA: Someone else. Are you really in love?

TESS *(shyly and warily)*: I am . . .

URSULA: A more burning passion than ours was?

TESS: Different.

URSULA: Do you ever dream about me?

TESS (*evasively*): Sometimes . . .

URSULA: I dreamt about you last night . . . intense and devastating details. Real passion.

TESS (*uneasy, interrupting*): Perhaps because of our plan. One often dreams about things discussed just before.

URSULA: Or desired.

TESS (*wants to avoid a disturbing subject*): She's waiting downstairs at the bar. I told her to make sure she was noticed. (*Goes to the window.*) When I lower the curtain again, she'll come up.

URSULA (*Looking around the apartment*): She has good taste. (*Going closer.*) This painting is worth $100,000, at least. Is she very rich?

TESS: Billions. Her father is in oil – Texas. He also imports from Saudi Arabia. They say he makes $10,000 an hour.

URSULA: You've chosen well. You always do. Does she have jewelry in the house? Ready cash?

TESS: Jewels.

URSULA: And you know where they are.

TESS: I do.

URSULA: What are they worth?

TESS: Close to half a million, she says.

URSULA (*quietly, as she observes Tess*): You could take off with the jewels. No one has seen you here. We could meet in Florida or Mexico in about six months. (*Silence.*) What do you say? I'm still interested. Nothing can replace for me what we once had . . . We might try again.

TESS *(nervously)*: You're joking. There's a very different plan, remember?

URSULA: Where did you put him?

TESS: As planned, in his bed, naked.

URSULA: Naked? Did she undress him?

TESS: I did. She was afraid to touch him; she's very upset. What should we do now?

URSULA: Where's the gun?

TESS: On the bed. With Marisa's fingerprints on it.

URSULA: How come?

TESS: Things were not going exactly as foreseen. He made a proposition.

URSULA: What proposition?

TESS: Imagine! He offered himself as "third wheel."

URSULA: "Wheel?"

TESS: That's what he called himself. He accepted my going to bed with his wife, but he also wanted to join us.

URSULA *(caustic)*: How typically male! They're spineless. They always want to participate in one way or the other. If nothing else, just watching. Peeping Toms! Well, what happened then?

TESS: At first we tried to convince him to go and leave us here alone. It would have been best for all of us.

URSULA: I warned you. They don't give up easily.

TESS: His attitude was maddening. There was hatred in the air, you could almost see it and touch it, it was so thick.

URSULA: I know you.

TESS *(ignoring this)*: He was impossible. There he sat, and I let him talk, talk . . .

URSULA *(dryly)*: The obscene proposal . . .

TESS: At the right moment I took him by surprise and tried to strangle him with my belt.

URSULA: Where is it?

TESS: Here. I was having a bad time at a certain point. He was strong, he was getting away from me. Marisa got my gun and fired.

URSULA: Voluntarily? On her own initiative?

TESS: Yes. She loves me. She did it because of that love. What are we going to do now?

(Ursula makes herself comfortable on the sofa in the same spot where Eugene was killed. It is a symbolic gesture, a challenge. She takes a notebook, a pen, and a gun from her bag. The gun is placed on the table, and she then consults her notebook.)

URSULA *(to Tess, slowly)*: The most logical thing. We have the woman's prints on the gun. Let's face the facts.

TESS: That is?

URSULA: She killed him because of jealousy.

TESS: Jealousy of whom?

URSULA *(takes a stocking and a pair of women's underpants from her bag)*: Anyone. The wife finds them together. She shoots. The other woman escapes leaving behind some evidence. Disappears, never to be found again. The wife will get away with a few hours in the lockup. Her father puts up bail. A sensational trial, it'll make the front page on every newspaper. She'll be acquitted, of course, as a defender of women's rights. She'll become the sensation of the day. A Star!

TESS: No trial. She's too vulnerable. She couldn't take it.

URSULA: I see. You don't want her to become a celebrity. (*Returns the underwear to her bag.*) Next possibility. Remove her fingerprints from the gun. Add your fingerprints instead. You fired in order to save her from her husband's vicious sadism. You'll be the one on trial. She'll pay expenses. You become the star.

TESS: No, she would have to testify. She'd mess everything up! She'd give us away.

URSULA: She's a genius, I see. Her heart is bigger than her brain, it seems. Suicide! He saw himself naked in the mirror and realized he was a nothing . . . (*Goes to the bedroom door and glances at the body.*) I thought so. A born impotent. He goes to the bed, settles himself carefully, and shoots. What do you think?

TESS: You told me to send her to the bar where she would be seen and noticed by possible witnesses. Why do that if it was suicide? It's obvious that you have another plan. What is it?

URSULA (*ignores this*): A suicide shocks. She went to the bar for a drink, trying to understand what happened. Of course she is pale and upset. She comes back, calls you, her only friend. You call me. We've known each other a long time. They'll believe it.

TESS: Two shots from a distance of at least six feet? That's suicide?

URSULA: No suicide, then. Show me the belt you strangled him with.

TESS: Tried to strangle. (*Hands her the belt.*) Here.

URSULA (*examines it*): Good strong leather. Are there any marks on his neck?

TESS: Very few. Almost invisible.

URSULA: We could add some S and M. We'll tie them together on the bed. I'll give her a few light bruises.

TESS: You don't touch Marisa.

URSULA: Why not?

TESS: Because I said "no."

URSULA *(scathingly)*: Her skin too delicate?

TESS *(avoiding the subject)*: Why tie her up too?

URSULA *(half seriously)*: While they're both tied up in there, maybe we can relive some of that wonderful past, you and I together here . . .

TESS: Please don't joke about this. This is the most serious day of my entire life.

URSULA: Oh, I like to think there was another day, in the past. You told me then it had been the most beautiful of your entire life. When we first met at that concert.

TESS: Yes, that's true. Everything I told you then was true. But now let's be serious. Why do you want to tie her up too?

URSULA: After undressing her.

TESS: Why?

URSULA: It should be obvious. I'm jealous. I'd like to check over my rival, to see . . .

TESS *(breaks in)*: Please stop this fooling. Were you serious when you suggested tying her together with him?

URSULA: I was.

TESS: For what reason?

URSULA: To teach her something. For your sake. Leave her next to her victim for a while. She'd never dare to even think of killing you after being forced to see the changes in a corpse. *(Dramatically.)* Violent death, muscular contractions, horror!

TESS: And then?

URSULA: In the meanwhile we'd have some time to discuss our situation.

TESS: Which situation?

URSULA: Ours. You and I. Let me tell you outright what might be the best solution.

TESS: Might be, if necessary. Go ahead.

URSULA: A bird in hand, or better, jewels in your hand are to be preferred to . . .

TESS (*interrupting*): No! I've already said no. Why don't you shoot him yourself?

URSULA: Shoot whom?

TESS: Him, there, in the bedroom. There's no trace of anything in this room. We can plant some clues in there. An officer has the right to carry out justice, with impunity, within the law.

URSULA: With impunity?

TESS: It happens. The gun is yours, the one you gave me once. You could say you were defending her — or that it was self-defense. They'd believe you.

URSULA (*thinks for a moment*): That gun is not registered in my name. It was never mine. I found it in a park.

TESS: Nice gifts you give me. Things you find in the bushes.

URSULA: It was a lovely garden, roses without thorns.

TESS (*ignoring this*): The story would hold up. You found the gun. You used it on a sadist who was torturing his wife. I would even permit . . .what you proposed before . . .

URSULA: Which is?

TESS: A few bruises on Marisa's semi-nude body . . .

URSULA: "Semi-nude?"

TESS: Whatever. You decide.

URSULA *(thinking it over)*: It's risky, might be suspect, it could ruin my career.

TESS: And save my life.

URSULA: I want to save it, and I could if I may suggest the simplest and easiest procedure, one which reduces the number of witnesses.

TESS: What is it?

URSULA: She's a beautiful woman, I grant you. But, as I gather from you, she's weak, vulnerable, insecure. She'll betray herself, she'll betray you.

TESS: Go on.

URSULA: You will end up in jail. I will not be able to help you. I will lose you.

TESS: I accept my risks.

URSULA: I care about you, about your future. Let them wallow in their own mud . . . *(Hesitates.)*

TESS: Keep talking.

URSULA: She killed him, and then committed suicide.

TESS: No!

URSULA: She's mentally ill. A perfect candidate for suicide.

TESS: And you're the one to persuade her to kill herself!

URSULA: I'll take care of it.

TESS: I know you. You would "suicide" her.

URSULA: I'll take care of it.

TESS *(explodes)*: You still don't understand, Ursie! I did love you once, intensely, deeply. Now I love her. She's adorable. Vulnerable, yes. Exquisitely feminine. She discovered joy with me. She's found life, love, pleasure. She's something completely new to me; she's sincere, naive, touching. She's mine, do you understand? My creation. She's daughter, sis-

ter, lover, she's everything to me! Help me, I beg
of you! For the sake of our really beautiful past. You
were everything to me then. She is everything to
me now. Help me, for the sake of our love, our
passion!

URSULA: "Our."

TESS: Yours and mine, yes, the past. And now . . .

URSULA (*breaks in, not wanting to hear anymore*):
Enough!

TESS (*her eyes on Ursula during a short silence*): I'm
pleading with you, Ursie . . . (*Kisses her hand.*)

URSULA (*apparently decided*): All right. You've convinced me. Lower the curtain. Let her come up.

TESS (*believes her, gives her a kiss*): Thank you, Ursie. (*She
runs to the window and lowers the curtain.*)

URSULA: Give me the belt. I'll tie him to the bed by
the neck. That'll account for the bruises. (*Tess gives
her the belt.*) And another thing. I still have the
letters and the love poems you wrote me. Knowing
you, I'm sure you've done the same with her. Where
are they?

TESS (*vaguely*): I don't know . . .

URSULA: You gave them to her yourself. No envelopes
therefore. Did you sign them?

TESS: Yes.

URSULA: Where are they?

TESS: In this house, of course, but I don't know where.

URSULA: Look for them. Meanwhile, I'll take care of
him.

(*Holding out the belt, Ursula goes into the bedroom. Tess
waits until she is sure that Ursula cannot see her, then
goes to a painting. She moves it and discloses a wall safe
behind it. She opens the safe easily and removes a packet*

of letters on blue paper. She hesitates. Returns them to the safe and closes it. She then goes around the room, opens drawers here and there, making enough noise to indicate to Ursula that she is searching. Ursula comes back into the room.)

URSULA: Have you found them?

TESS: No.

URSULA: They shouldn't remain here. We'll ask your woman where they are.

(A key is heard in the lock, then footsteps. Marisa enters looking shy, unsure, and ill at ease. Tess goes to her and embraces her.)

TESS: All in order. This is my friend Ursula. She's going to help us.

URSULA *(holds out her hand with a big smile)*: Hello, Marisa. Don't worry. Everything will work out fine. Sit down. I need to know some details. *(Marisa sits down timidly. Ursula prepares to take notes.)*

URSULA: What year were you married?

MARISA *(still anxious and uncertain)* Seven years ago.

URSULA: Tess told me about it: it was a difficult, joyless marriage. *(Marisa nods.)* A cruel insensitive man.

(Marisa looks at Tess anxiously and questioningly. Tess motions to her to reply affirmatively.)

MARISA *(weakly)*: Yes.

URSULA: A crude vulgar man. He married you for your money. *(Tess signals to Marisa to agree. Marisa is unsure.)*

MARISA *(indecisively)*: At the beginning, he was . . .

URSULA *(taking it up)*: . . . more human, more decent. They're all like that. *(Pause.)* Now a personal question. I won't write down your answer, but it's important for me to know. Is it true that you never, never experienced pleasure? Never enjoyed it?

MARISA *(looking down uneasily)*: I don't understand.

URSULA: Tess told me everything. You know very well what I'm talking about. Is it true or not?

MARISA *(barely audible)*: True.

URSULA: And that for the first time in your life you experienced joy when making love with our friend Tess? *(Silence. Marisa has trouble answering.)* Look, I'm not writing this down? Is it true? *(Marisa nods timidly.)* Good. Now tell me what happened today. *(Marisa looks at her in surprise.)* Tess did explain everything, and I believe her. But in my profession, we need different points of view. I need your version. *(Marisa looks at Tess who nods.)*

TESS: She knows everything. I told her the truth. You can speak.

MARISA: I confirm everything.

URSULA: In your own words.

MARISA *(unsure)*: I told him that I didn't love him anymore. He seemed to understand. I thought he had accepted, then he met Tess, he changed his mind.

URSULA: I understand why.

MARISA *(doubtfully, searching for the right words)*: Then he suggested . . .

URSULA: What?

MARISA: Something horrible . . . obscene . . .

URSULA: And that was?

(Marisa can't answer. Tess intervenes.)

TESS: I've explained all that. He proposed a threesome. It was at that moment that . . .

(She motions to Marisa. Marisa doesn't know how to continue.)

TESS: . . . she was forced to shoot. Then we carried him in there, according to your instructions. You've seen him. What do we do now?

URSULA: One step at a time. *(To Marisa.)* Tess tells me that she wrote you love letters and dedicated poems she wrote to you. *(Her eyes steadily on her.)* Is this true?

MARISA *(faintly)*: Yes.

URSULA: They can't remain in this house. Give them to Tess.
(Marisa goes to the safe, opens it, and hands the letters to Tess, who appears tense and nervous for the first time.)

URSULA *(inquisitively)*: How come they were there? Couldn't your husband have found them?

MARISA: That's my personal safe. He doesn't know — *(corrects herself)* — didn't know the combination.

URSULA: You're using the past tense for the first time. You'll get used to it.

MARISA: He kept his things in that cabinet.
(Tess walks towards the piece, wanting to be helpful.)

URSULA: His things are of no interest here. *(Tess stops.)*

URSULA *(to Marisa)*: Do you have anything else of Tess's?

MARISA *(thinking)*: No.

URSULA: Better that way. *(To Tess, pointing to the letters she still holds.)* Put them here. *(Indicates the table. Tess is reluctant.)* That way you'll remember to take them to your apartment. Nothing should be found here that might link the two of you in any way.
(Tess puts the letters on the table.)

URSULA: I saw the gun over there. *(To Marisa.)* It's got

your fingerprints. I didn't touch it. Now, this is the plan. You will say that you got home . . . *(looks at her watch)* . . . at about five o'clock. You heard sounds from the bedroom. You approached without making a sound and found your husband in bed with another woman. You ran out to the bar, you were shocked and disturbed. Who saw you?

MARISA: The doorman downstairs, the bartender, some people at the bar.

URSULA: Excellent. Were you calm and composed?

MARISA: Absolutely not. I was trembling and pale. I ordered a brandy and drank it in one gulp. I hate alcohol. I went to the phone twice, wanting to call Tess . . .

URSULA: A perfect alibi. You will tell the truth then. What you did at the bar, and then how you came back here. That, as you hesitated at the front door, you heard two shots. You rushed in and saw the woman running out of the bedroom with a gun in her hand. *She* killed your husband. She escaped leaving only this behind. *(She shows the stocking and underwear which she has taken out of her bag again.)* The woman has disappeared. You are in the clear.

(Tess smiles. It seems a good solution to her.)

URSULA: What do you think?

TESS *(as Marisa nods)*: Perfect! Thanks!

URSULA: Let's do a general run-through to work out timing. *(To Marisa.)* You go out into the hall. *(To Tess, handing her a handkerchief.)* You rub off the fingerprints from the gun. When I clap my hands twice, that will be the two shots, you come in from the right and you from the left. Marisa will be

frightened and shaky. Tess, you threaten her with the gun, then run out. Let's try it.
(The two women go out, one to the right and into the bedroom, the other left, into the hall. Ursula remains alone; she takes out her gun and places it on the table.)

URSULA *(loudly)*: Tess are you ready with the gun?

TESS *(from the bedroom)*: Ready.

(A moment of tension.)

URSULA: Listen carefully now. I'm ready. The two shots. *(Ursula claps her hands twice. Marisa comes in from the hall. Tess comes in from the bedroom with the gun in one hand and the handkerchief in the other.)* Good. Keep going. *(Now Marisa goes toward Tess. Tess instinctively points the gun at Marisa. Ursula picks up her gun and fires at Tess, killing her. Marisa stands motionless, petrified. Slowly and deliberately)* She threatened you. It was my duty to defend you. *(Picks up her handkerchief and puts it in her pocket.)* Marisa, she admitted to me that she only wanted your money. I couldn't let her take advantage of you like that, and get away with it. We'll tell them exactly what we decided before, with one difference. You came back from the bar with me, we came in here together. We heard two shots, then she *(indicating Tess)* came out of the bedroom with the gun pointed at us. I had to shoot her. You are not to blame in any way. You're merely the victim of your husband and of that woman. I'll take care of you, Marisa. You have nothing to fear. *(Points to Tess and then to the letters on the table.)* I was once her lover and teacher. Whatever she knew she learned from me. Don't worry about anything, Marisa. I'm here now in your life. I'll protect you. I'll take care of you with love. *(She picks up the letters and presses them to her heart.)*

Curtain